A TOUCHSTONE OF
IMPACT

A TOUCHSTONE OF
IMPACT

The Life of Linda Eatmon-Jones

STEVE EATMON

XULON PRESS

Xulon Press
2301 Lucien Way #415
Maitland, FL 32751
407.339.4217
www.xulonpress.com

Paperback ISBN-13: 978-1-6628-1483-9

Ebook ISBN-13: 978-1-6628-1484-6

Dedicated to my beautiful wife, Heather, and our wonderful children Ryan and Rachael – may the memory of Grammy be forever strong in your lives.

RIP Mom, 1948-2020

TABLE OF CONTENTS

INTRODUCTION ix

CHAPTER 1: THE CAR RIDE. 1
CHAPTER 2: FAMILY LIFE 9
CHAPTER 3: IMPACT AT CHURCH. 37
CHAPTER 4: WORK LIFE 61
CHAPTER 5: FRIENDS AND COLLEAGUES. 77
CHAPTER 6: THE NEXT GENERATION. .93
CHAPTER 7: IMPACT ON ME. 103

EPILOGUE 117
ACKNOWLEDGEMENTS 131
REFERENCES 133

INTRODUCTION

That day, it was a Sunday, will never fade from my memory. Mid-spring and we were in the heart of April. Everyone was glad the sun had finally shown itself. We and the world were living in a new lifestyle. We'd adjusted, somewhat, to pandemic life. Under the rules of our old lives, most days were hectic, running here and there, exchanging pleasantries, getting ready for a sermon, a Sunday School lesson, or a meeting. But now days had been marked by tranquility, a peacefulness, perhaps even too great a calm. We'd set up the laptop to watch church online, everyone gathered on the deck because of the nice weather. Afterward, we hiked and explored the trails around the neighborhood. Mid-afternoon, we had a family zoom call scheduled. We returned from the family walk and quickly got the kids ready for the zoom call. We settled in the living room and dialed in.

Cousins joined the call, and then Auntie entered the virtual room. We exchanged pleasantries and our young children showcased their animals and toys. A growing concern entered my mind as I waited for my mother and step-father to log into the call. "Could there be technical problems?" I asked. "They had some problems last time." But as minutes wore on, this theory quickly morphed from a sense of confusion to a sense of worry and then to deep-seated inner panic – the sinking feeling you get in your stomach when you know something is seriously wrong.

Twelve minutes past the appointed time, I stepped aside, into another room, picked up the phone and called. First I tried my mother, *no answer*, then my stepfather's phone. Three rings, then the connection was established. The several minutes-long response that would serve to permanently alter the course of this family's history and future.

"Are you having problems logging into the call?" I asked.

"Actually, your mother had to go to the emergency room." I heard the worry in his voice. "She was in a lot of pain and was weak. I called an ambulance and followed it to the hospital. They won't let me in because of Covid-19, but the doctor will call me as soon as they get an update." A discussion ensued between my stepdad and I over whether or not to tell anyone on the zoom call or just it persist without breaking the news, but it would be hard to carry on regardless.

A rather awkward exchange resumed on the zoom call, pretending to be calm and present a demeanor of normalcy, but the tension finally broke. I explained that Mom needed to go to the hospital, and she needed prayer. I knew from a phone call the day before that her cancer had returned. The added delay in getting results of her MRI test, due to the lack of available medical staff in the pandemic, contributed to the growth. She didn't sound as ready to take on the challenge as she had with the first bout six years before, but nonetheless said she would keep treading and could still convince a skeptic she would overcome. None of us, however, were prepared for the occurrences during the next few days.

To say that the seventy-two-hour journey in the hospital became excruciating would be an understatement. No visitation was allowed. We just waited for a phone call from the doctor or the nurse. What we were given was piercing news of Mom's failing health – a downhill roller coaster traversing from concern to shock to the realization that we may have seen the last of the dynamic, ebullient force of nature known as Linda Eatmon-Jones. Two days after her admission, wanting a call to know what is happening, but at the same time wishing it wouldn't for fear of more bad news, my smartphone vibrated. It was my step-father, who put the doctor on the phone to break the paralyzing news. "I'm sorry, sir, but we have tried everything. There is nothing we can do to save your mother."

I hung up. I banged the door. I called back and pleaded with the medical staff to bring my family on the fifty-minute trek from our home in upper Montgomery County, MD, to the hospital in Fairfax, VA.

We all went, not even knowing if we would be allowed into the hospital. Upon arrival, we receive the rules of engagement, *only two at a time could enter.* I could visit, my kids could come. This was good news, provided we all passed the temperature checks and wore a mask. I signed in, thankful for good health habits instilled by my wife as the hospital thermometer gun scanned on my forehead read 97.3. I took the escalator, moved with purpose toward the hospital room only to see a sight that will burn in my head for decades as a sleep-inhibiting vision. The strong-willed, fiery, always active spirit of my mother was rendered completely helpless. She lay still with IV needles stuck in her veins and a breathing tube lodged in her mouth. She exhaled loudly and laboriously in what is known as "the death growl." I recognized it from my grandmother, who'd passed just fifty-two days earlier.

There would be no conversations in that room. It was too late for that. The last communication will be remembered as her telling me she was getting medicated and would call me back. Now I could just talk without knowing how my words would be received. There would be no reply. My aunt called and prayed aloud over the speakerphone for a miracle. I remember Mom's weakened hand making an attempt to grab mine in what would be her final gesture before passing the next day.

No one – not even the medical staff – thought that when she left the home she had poured her heart into for twenty-three years, that Sunday afternoon, that she would never see it again. It was such an abrupt, premature end to a life that left so many unanswered questions: Why now? We thought she was healthy enough to see life well into her nineties. Who knew she was that sick? Did she know that she was that sick? What signs had we missed? She made it a point not to worry anyone about her failing health. But one fact remained through it all – what was left behind was a life of impact. "She lived until she died" is an oft-used cliché, but here it rang true: a life spent living on one's own terms, a life of fighting, of overcoming the odds, a life defined by influence whose legacy will live on.

In this book, you will see first-hand the impact that was left in the seventy-two years that my mother walked this earth, and you will hear it through those she impacted. In 2015, she approached me, and many others about working on a book commemorating the influence of my step-father, a collection of essays from the perspective of those he touched. The book, released in the summer of 2016, went on to win an EVVY award. In a similar fashion, through this work, you will see from the perspective of those she touched, how my mother inspired, influenced, and impacted her world

Through Their Eyes

There are five definitions for the word *impact* in the dictionary, but when describing it within the context of Linda Eatmon-Jones' life, one stands out above the rest: *influence; effect.* This book is but an attempt to quantify the influence and impact of her life.

There is no cut and dry way to measure influence. It can be breath: the number of people who adopt a saying, a habit, or a lifestyle. It can be depth: the amount of influence a certain individual adopts from the one who influences. It can be the amount of systemic change within an institution, an industry or organization as a result of an individual. But for my mother, you will see a mixture of all of the above from the different types of people with whom she came in contact.

There is an assumption that a life of impact is one lived by a celebrity or someone well-known on a public scale. Often times when students in a school are asked to name someone they look up to or admire, the oft-quoted answer is a famous person that they have never met. But more frequently, I believe, our influence comes from those around us. It is true that the impact of certain public figures can instill lasting institutional change on the framework by which people live, but our beliefs, our habits, our actions, our speech, are shaped, consciously or unconsciously, by those in whom we have regular contact.

In the wake of my mother's passing, two themes emerged. First, she died too soon. Even though Psalm 90:10 tells us "Our days may come to 70 years," and mom died at 72, when someone lives life a certain way and touches other lives in the process, the tacit expectation is that they should be able to earn more years in the process.

Second, some have uttered the phrase, "She lived life to the fullest." It is a trite phrase that can often seem overused and cliché, but as you will see from these essays, that mantra will ring true. She was full of life – an honored family matriarch, and a doting grandmother. Mom characterized a relentlessly hard-working employee and businesswoman. She embodied an interpersonal force who could easily connect with a sanitation worker coming to do a pickup as well as the CEO of a multinational corporation, an event planner, an award-winning writer, or a horticulturist who could host an HGTV show. Mom had always been a godly woman who contributed to raising children and grandchildren in the Christian faith.

Her loss was felt by many, and this book is the outlet for those to express not only what they have lost, but more importantly, gained during the years she lived.

This book is a combination of essays and feedback submitted by those who knew her, those whose lives she affected. Linda's world was varied and diverse throughout her years. Though she only lived in two states throughout her life, North Carolina and Virginia, her relationships, networks, and influence have traversed continents.

The works are split into sections, based on the types of relationships, with an introduction and the works of those within each strata of relationship.

After setting the scene and giving you, as the reader, background and context in Chapter 1, you will begin to see the essays of influence from those she touched beginning in Chapter 2, which are divided into four sections in four chapters. The sections are family life, work/community development, friends, and impact on the next generation. Though these essays are divided into sections, one cannot possibly compartmentalize Linda's life. In actuality, just about everyone should be listed under the category of family, because whether you were a friend, a co-worker, or a colleague, you were family to her. However, I did the painstaking work of trying to surgically separate, as much as possible,

The outline of each section is as follows: an introduction briefly describing her life, work, and relationships in the given area, and the essays written by those who were part of that area of Linda's life, categorized alphabetically. A total of forty-eight essays have been collected, sixteen of family life, fourteen from church, six in work, ten from friends, and two for the next generation.

Chapter 1
THE CAR RIDE

I was sixteen years old, and it was another ordinary run-of-the-mill trip "down south" as many of my relatives call it, to my mother's hometown of Ahoskie, North Carolina. She and I made trips frequently. Even though I grew up in northern Virginia, I still take my wife and kids down there frequently to know their heritage. The trips are usually a round-robin of visitations with relatives and people who were influential during my mother's upbringing. Ahoskie is a small town with a small-town mentality. Everyone knows each other (not literally everyone, but most people), helps each other, and always made time for family, especially visitors from out of town.

I was with Mom in the car, leaving Ahoskie to head home. As we traveled along Highway 13 – the main thoroughfare in town, she decided to stop and see someone at the local community college, a man by the name of Harold Mitchell, who she described as "someone I knew from way back when." After the brief meeting in which I learned he was her cousin, the next few minutes in the car became a seismic shift in the foundation of how I viewed my family and myself.

"So how is Harold related to us?" I casually asked.

"I need to tell you something," she said. Her the tone was not one of "I am in trouble" but more like a secret or some kind of serious health problem.

Brewing within me was a mix of intrigue, concern, and borderline fear of what would come next.

"George is not actually my daddy." She talked without pause, implicitly understanding the next breath out of my mouth would be "Well, who is?" Or maybe I'd perceive, "Well, I just spent the last sixteen years lying to friends, teachers, and even family members."

So my family history I had rehearsed to so many, "I never knew my grandfather, he died from cancer a few years before I was born, but I heard he was a good, hard-working man," now gave way to a flood of questions. "Is my grandmother really my grandmother? What about my aunts, uncles, and cousins? Whose family am I a part of? Maybe my grandfather is actually alive, where can I meet him?"

She went on, "I never knew my father, Peter Williams. He left before I was even born. Grammy (my grandmother) never really spoke to him after she became pregnant with me, so don't ever bring up the subject around her. They were together briefly, but it was an illicit relationship not approved by all parties, and when she became pregnant, he skipped town and went to the Norfolk-Virginia Beach area, where he stayed until his death in 1973. A few months after I was born, your grandmother met George and they got married, so your other aunts and uncles are the product of George and your grandmother but not me. And Harold is my father's first cousin."

Well, this would take some processing.

Even more bizarre was the story of my mother's birth. A woman as unique as my mother, who had such a unique way with people and one-of-a-kind impact on those she touched, had to have an entrance in this world that is a story for the generations.

My grandmother, all by herself, as a black woman in the south in the late 1940s, was about to give birth. She called the doctor as the contractions came. The doctor, a white man, pulled up to the house in a black neighborhood. This was the racially segregated Jim Crow South. He drove a car that everyone in that neighborhood could only dream of acquiring. And, in almost expected fashion, while he was attending to the birth, two boys from the neighborhood seized the opportunity and stole his car, dashing out of the neighborhood. In an even more typical fashion, the white doctor – in the middle of performing a childbirth – left the black woman in labor to pursue the boys who have stolen his prized possession. As I said, this was the Jim Crow South, in the 1940s. That was how things were in those days.

That event created a mix-up of vital records. Doctors performing home births in small towns completed the paperwork at the time. I had always assumed my mother's birthday to be March 2, the date she told me when I was young. It took many years for her to receive a birth certificate and when asked, of course, the recollection of dates were not exact. "Most likely sometime between February 24 and March 8," was the given answer, but how many birth certificates printed in town hall records have ranges on them? An exact date had to be given, and the easiest solution? Choose the date in the middle, March 2.

HUMBLE BEGINNINGS

Linda grew up in small-town America, a place where neighbors were always willing to help and everyone knew your name – it is hard to hide in a place like Ahoskie. So naturally, word about these kinds of events spread. It became apparent as she grew up that she was different from her brothers and sisters, and people sometimes treated her as such.

During the 1950s and 1960s, a child born out of wedlock was called an illegitimate child, a label that was hard to break and often influenced a child's destiny. She was introduced to that label in the fifth grade when some cousins mentioned this to her while walking home from school. Even though her mother Viola met a man named George Harrell just a few years later and the two were later married, many of the stigmas of her birth still resonated.

There was always a sense that George's family did not accept her as their own, even though George did. For example, they would refer to her sisters as "Daddy's wife's children." Cousins wouldn't allow her to play with them, and she doesn't recall being referred to with a family title such as granddaughter, niece, or cousin, but just referred to by name. An excerpt from her book, *Thank You Daddy,* sheds some more light on this unfortunate situation.

> *Perhaps the biggest "slap in the face" was when Daddy's (George's) sister gave birth to her first daughter just after he married my mother. His sister named her daughter my exact name – both first and middle – which was and still is highly unusual in a family for kids so close in age and we were not namesakes of a family elder. She was making a statement that I could not even have my own name in his family – it had to be owned by her daughter. It created so much confusion because we were only three years apart in age. While I was in college, his mother passed and his family only wanted my name listed in the obituary as Daddy's stepdaughter with no connection to their mother even though Daddy had adopted me by that time.* [1]

Unfortunate beginnings can take a person in one or two directions – situations can break them, cause them to retreat into the realm of defeat, create a never-resolved crisis of identity or cause a person to resent themselves their parents and the unfortunate events of their background. Or it can *make them*. In this event, the person will form a steel-like resolve that inoculates a person to the potentially destructive nature of trials and allows them to see with a perspective of possibility and creativity instead of limitation. For Linda, it was the latter, as quoted by the Mayor of Ahoskie, NC, when elaborating on the famous quote "when life give you lemons, make lemonade." He then remarked, "She didn't just make lemonade, she gave you the recipe." That is the measure of deep impact – a few, when given the lemons will have the resolve to make the lemonade, which is extremely admirable in and of itself, but out of those few, even fewer will go on to teach others how to do the same.

As mentioned earlier, while Linda was still an infant, her mother Viola met a man named George Harrell and the two were later married. This was a much-needed break at a crucial age, a stable two-parent household to provide direction, accountability, and everything else. Much of the nature of this relationship was described in her second book, *Thank You Daddy*. While it is possible that one can become a socially and emotionally stable human being in this world without a father and go on to live a life of impact, the odds of success are slim without a stable father figure throughout childhood. Here are some statistics that demonstrate this phenomenon:

- Children living with both biological parents are 20 to 35 percent more physically healthy than children from broken homes (Dawson).[2]

- Children growing up in homes where two parents who have been married, continuously, are less likely to experience a wide range of problems (academic, social, emotional, cognitive), not only in childhood but later on in adulthood as well (Amato; Howard & Reeves).[2]

- Research also shows that family intactness has a beneficial influence on reducing out-of-wedlock births, increasing high school and college graduation rates, and even has long-term benefits such as higher employment rates (Amato; Howard & Reeves).[2]

Statistics such as these have plagued the black community and contributed to a vicious cycle of emotional and social instability reflected in three major areas. (1) Poor role models for emotional development and conflict management skills leading to violent and sexually promiscuous behavior. (2) A lack of fiscal responsibility prevents the building of long-term generational wealth that ends the cycle of poverty. (3) An under-emphasis on education, which allows one to create and develop employable skills that lead to long-term financial stability.

The presence and investment of a father in his children's lives is of paramount importance and was a key contributor to my mother avoiding these three pitfalls of African-American youth.

MAKING LEMONS OUT OF LEMONADE

Linda graduated as the valedictorian of her class in 1965 from Robert L. Vann High School in Ahoskie, NC, and in 1969 from North Carolina Central University with a double major in psychology and mathematics. The 1960s were marked with turbulence related to race relations and the Vietnam war. Her credentials would have taken her much further in the twenty-first century, but in those days she was limited to education from all-black, segregated schools. Black students were integrated into the formerly all-white Ahoskie High School in 1970, and though her academic resume could have afforded her admittance into Duke and the University of North Carolina – Chapel Hill, predominantly white schools at the time, her chances of admission were slim. Still, the old adage rang true for Linda – if life gives you lemons, make lemonade.

For many blacks to have succeeded in the mid-twentieth century (and in many cases, even still today), they had to learn how to make lemons out of lemonade. That's just what Linda did. She graduated from North Carolina Central University and landed a job programming the original mainframe computers. Her career led her out of the Carolinas and into the Northern Virginia suburbs of the Washington, DC area in the early 1970s.

It was from there that she would live out the rest of her days, about a half-century's worth, raising a family, obtaining two master's Degrees from Harvard University in Cambridge, MA and George Mason University in Fairfax, VA. She worked in the corporate and non-profit sector and served faithfully in her church and community. And it was there, where her greatest impact would be felt, as a businesswoman, a community leader, a devoted wife, mother, grandmother, family member, and friend, and in the final years, an award-winning author.

There is a lot more I can say about her life, but you, as the reader, will find out through the words of those she touched. After all, that is the point of this book. It is time that I turn the page over to the others whose lives she touched and influenced.

Chapter 2
FAMILY LIFE

"Family is not an important thing – it's everything." –
Michael J. Fox[4]

This chapter shows an array of essays written by those who were family members. For Linda, everyone was essentially family, but for the purposes of this section, which was no easy task, I separated out those who were naturally or legally considered relatives.

Linda was extremely devoted to her family and a fierce believer in strong family values as a means for success in life. The strongest support mechanism for any individual is their family. The outside world can only do so much to help you, so the family must provide the lion's share of a child's (and adult's) development in life. Families provide not just the tangible things that people see – shelter, food, water, and basic physical necessities, but many intangible things as well – emotional health, psychological well-being, and sound spiritual development. A recent study[3] from Pew Research found that 80 percent of teens (ages 13-17) whose parents are evangelical, maintain their religious identity, while 81 percent of teens from Catholic homes share their parents' religious views. The family is a vital institution necessary for the development of the whole person. Linda was a staunch believer in this.

From Linda's first book, *Touchstone*, she mentioned her main principles that she and her husband Earle lived by as family members.

- Family will give you the love you need without you having to force it out of them

- Your family will always tell you the truth, whether or not you want the honest truth. One may have gotten the typical, "Take that outfit off right now," and the "You were 100-percent wrong." Even if the truth was not sought, you got it and for that, be thankful and grateful for honesty

- Think of the worst situation and the best situation, and then think of the people who would really be there next to you. Your family, for both – through thick and thin are your best supporters.

- Family relationships teach you a set of morals and principles that you take with you to use to survive in the real world – ethical and spiritual guidance.[4]

Being African-American, Linda was especially passionate about strong family values since there is an epidemic of broken families among the African-American culture in the past few decades. Examining the cause is a complex process, but the statistics are staggering.

- In 1960, just 22 percent of black children were raised in single-parent families. Fifty years later, in 2010, more than 70 percent of black children were raised in single-parent families.[5]

- According to the 1938 Encyclopedia of the Social Sciences, that year, 11 percent of black children were born to unwed mothers. Today, about 75 percent of black children are born to unwed mothers.[5]

- The percentage of white children under eighteen who live with both parents almost doubles that of black children, according to the data. While 74.3 percent of all white children below the age of eighteen live with both parents, only 38.7 percent of African-American minors can say the same. (US Census Bureau)[6]

These essays will show the impact Linda had on her relatives and her willingness and commitment to keep a healthy family structure. You will see a diverse array of writings from immediate family members, extended family members, and in-laws. Being born out of wedlock herself to a father she never knew, Linda was adopted as a small child by her stepfather. However, she rediscovered her birth father's family and became a very involved and committed member. It would have been very easy to maintain bitterness and resentment and refrain from developing relationships with that side of the family out of fear of discomfort, but for Linda, that didn't matter.

I remember going with her to our first Mitchell-Newsome family reunion during Labor Day weekend of 2003. The greeting we received was extremely warm, and we instantly knew that we had a "new" family. Linda continued to develop relationships with that side of the family to the point where she herself became an integral part in planning the reunions that took place every other year. She also took the time to trace the complete Mitchell-Newsome lineage five generations back to the original patriarch and matriarch – Junius Mitchell and Aurora Newsome. The ancestors' information was displayed at the 2017 family reunion, so that everyone there could find their true place in the family. Though Linda was a hard worker, family came first and it showed in all she did.

The following are the family members who have written essays about Linda's impact on their lives.

Yvonne Delevoye (Niece)
Laurent Delevoye (Nephew-in-law)
Paul, Alexandre and Samuel Delevoye (Great Nephews)
Naweal Demery (Great Niece)
Heather Eatmon (Daughter-in-law)
James Eatmon (First Husband)
Shontese Harrell-Ford (Niece)
Kimberly Harrell-Mills (Niece)
Earle Jones (Second Husband)
James Mitchell (Cousin)
Priscilla Mitchell (Cousin)
Gloria (Doby) Parker (Cousin)
James and Mary Simmons (in-laws, parents of Heather
Eatmon, daughter-in-law)
Corelette Smith (Sister)
Sylvia Turrell (Sister-in-Law)
Teri Britt Watts (Cousin)

Laurent Delevoye (Nephew-in-law)

You had a gift.
You could see into a person's heart.
Because you looked beyond the physical appearance, you could set aside cultural and social differences.
You never forgot a birthday. Often, you organized gift-opening events.
Your gifts made everyone feel honored and, through these small gestures, you knew how to make everyone feel important.
Even thousands of miles away, you and Uncle Earle helped us raise our kids.

You observed, encouraged, and confirmed our choices as young parents on the upbringing of our boys.
I will be forever grateful to you for embracing me in your lovely family cocoon.

Laurent

Paul, Alexandre, and Samuel Delevoye (Great Nephews)

Dear Aunt Linda,
Being at a distance in times like this is hard... especially since our only wish would be to hug you forever.
We will try to put words on our feelings, even if it feels as if we are putting limits on infinity.
We will miss the small secrets that we had only with you.
Our brains will work; our hearts will beat thinking of you and empowered with the love that you forever gave to each one of us.
We felt unstoppable when next to you, thanks to all the strength and love you spread.
You always took special care to our small and insignificant bruises. You never shared your problems, so that we would not get worried.
But words are powerless to describe the impact you have had on us as kids... as teenagers... and as young men!
Having you by our side was a blessing.
We will do our best to obey, adhering to the many things you taught us, keeping in mind your keys to a happy and simple life.

Farewell, Aunt Linda
Paul, Alexandre, and Samuel

Yvonne Delevoye (Niece)

Your energy was radiant
Your love was true
You helped me in so many ways, simply by opening your house to me at a time when I desperately needed to understand my roots, or to simply find myself again.

With patience, you helped me open my eyes and heart, and gave me the power to trust again.
Thank you.

Your office was the place to be!
We were always hesitant to walk in – afraid to bother you – but you always had time for us.
So many open heart discussions about everything and anything, as long as it was accurate, referenced, truthful!
Through the long hours of discussions, we would observe, listen, and learn.
I learned to understand the importance of timing—the art of knowing *when to say what*.
I have not mastered this art of public debating – far from it. But I know that from where ever you are – you are still guiding my steps.

Our last talk was about the half-smile – the importance of keeping a poker face in public places.
That simply won't be possible today.
My heart is crying.

You have left too soon, Aunt Linda, but your gifts are in our house and remain in our souls.

Yvonne

Naweal Demory (Great Niece)

Aunt Linda,

I will never forget you, never – you always remained so pretty and so sweet. I will never forget you. Even if we didn't see each other very often, you will stay forever deep in my heart. Uncle Earle, you really chose well.

Floods of kisses
Naweal

Heather Eatmon (Daughter-in-Law)

Linda's incredible energy was inspiring. In the first several years that I knew her, she was perpetually on her feet moving. Her hands were always busy with daily tasks, decorating her beautiful home, or helping someone in need.

As I dated her son, Steve, and got to know him better, I could see that she had made a great mark on his life. His rare mix of strength and independence, along with his kind, patient, and supportive nature, was surprising to encounter. I could see that the care she had for him had greatly shaped the man I grew to love.

When our son Ryan was born, she took the role of "Grammy" very seriously. Steve and I lived with her and Earle that year, and she offered to help with night feedings. She told me that at 3:00 am, she would care for Ryan so I could sleep. Since Ryan was often waking constantly through the night, that was a huge help!

She always made herself available for her grandchildren. She received a cancer diagnosis around the time that Rachael was born, but she continued to reach out as much as she was able. Thankfully, she later went into remission for several years and was able to enjoy wonderful times with Ryan and Rachael. Spending the night at Grammy and Grandad's was always a thrill for them. The children enjoyed delicious treats and their favorite foods at mealtimes. They had a fun playroom and each had their own colorful and inviting bedrooms. Coming to Grammy and Grandad's was like stepping into a castle where they were king and queen for the night. As the sign in the playroom said, "The answer is always 'Yes' at Grandma's!" When they had to come back down to earth, or home, sometimes there were many tears.

Linda had a way with words. If one of her grandchildren was having a difficult time, she often knew just what to say to help them to understand a complex situation or try a new challenge.

Her encouragement inspired great confidence in them. I am so thankful for the impact she has had on all of us.

James Eatmon (First Husband)

Linda Eatmon-Jones

I remember the first time I saw her. I was deep in thought, as computer programmers often are, gazing at the hallway across from my office when she walked past my door. My attention immediately

switched to her profile as she moved by for that brief second. It was her gait that struck me. Her body not fully upright but tilted slightly backward as if she couldn't keep up with her feet. She had her special smile oner face. She didn't look toward my door as most people would. She was a new employee selected among about half a dozen through some special government intern program. We met a short time later when she was sent to my office to be trained and assist me with a project I was working on. We became associates and a friendship was formed. It was so easy to share personal and intimate life experiences with her. As our friendship grew, I shared with her a personal problem I was having and had been a part of me since my teen years, that of anxiety and severe depression but not diagnosed as bi-polar.

Sometimes it was all I could do to struggle through the day and keep it hidden. I still have bouts of depression but I have learned to get past it reasonably well, but my condition I carried into our marriage. I was separated from my former wife and heading for divorce but had time, on occasion, to see Linda. Some months later, we began to see each other after work and began dating. She had ended a relationship with another man, a very nice employee where we worked and she wanted to move from Maryland to Virginia. I assisted her in locating a townhouse in Fairfax, Va. This was where we later lived following our marriage.

As my divorce became final and we grew much closer, she would often visit me at my apartment in Falls Church, Va. In the late 1970s, inter-racial marriage was still taboo. And one day in early 1979, she asked me to marry her and after discussion, we agreed to go our separate ways – but she came back a few days later and I knew I was hooked. During this time, her father was in hospital with colon cancer. She wanted me to visit him (I believe she wanted her dad to know that she had found someone to love). I drove her to Norfolk to hospital to see her dad. We met and talked and later I took her back home to her place in Fairfax. Her father died shortly afterwards and I accompanied her to his funeral and met her family. I had already met her sister, Jenny, some months before.

Throughout the years I was married to her, Linda was so naive and nonchalant about many things (so funny at times). At our wedding in April 1979, all our family and friends were present at the Baptist Church (and later at the reception in Arlington, VA) just down the street from her townhouse. I had my best man and groomsmen, but Linda didn't have anyone, neither bridesmaids or attendants. Later, she realized that she had forgotten that part of the ceremony and we had a good laugh. Shortly after we were married, I caught the flu, the worst case I've ever had. I had to go to hospital twice. In the middle of the flu, she came home with a new pair of shoes she had purchased for me. I still do not know why she thought that a new pair of shoes would help cure me. But I loved her for it.

I always enjoyed the hilarity of her somewhat reckless behavior at times. She told me the story of how she would drive from her parents' home in Ahoskie, NC to DC wearing nothing but a nightgown. She was also barefoot. And the time she had surgery on her toes and was wheeled into the hospital being pushed and riding on a flimsy supply cart.

Just months after we were married, she came home one day and said she had found the house she wanted to live in. We moved to Burke, VA, where we spent the last years of our marriage. It was there that we had a son. The night she went into labor and at the hospital while waiting for things to progress, our son decided to do a 180-degree turn in her womb and the doctor said he had to do a Caesarean extraction. This was the first time I was allowed to be present at my child's birth. Also, this was before ultrasound, so we didn't know the sex of our child. I remember talking to Linda as the procedure was ongoing and as our son was being pulled from his mother's body by his feet with only his head still inside her body. Then, he urinated on her. We later had a good laugh about that.

As time progressed in our marriage, my emotional problems peaked. The anxiety and depression increased. I would frequently awaken at night after frightening nightmares. Most nights, Linda did not know. I became sullen and aloof from her. My anxiety increased. In efforts to keep my pain from her and our son, I grew distant. I became hostile towards her at times. We discussed my tendency to possibly harm her and/or our son. We decided that it would be best if we lived apart. And we lived apart for about five years before our divorce. Fortunately, I eventually came to terms with my mental problems and today, I am nearly normal.

Linda was an inspiration to everyone she met. She was ambitious, devoted to those around her, caring, attentive, and interested in what others had to say. She always cared about those around her. I have never known anyone like her. *Unique* cannot describe the person she was, so rare a human being. She touched so many lives in wonderful and positive ways that cannot be expounded upon here. She was so special and will be sorely missed by those who knew her – Earle, her husband, our son and his wife, our grandchildren, me, and others so close. I will always be in love with Linda; she was the great love of my life.

I am profoundly glad that she had a wonderful husband for twenty-one years to complete her life. I always believed that she would live decades plus beyond my lifetime because she was so good a person, unlike anyone I have ever known. We will miss you Linda, for all the days of our lives.

Were I Pygmalion or God
I would make you exactly as you were...in all dimensions.
From your warm hair to your intimate toes would you be,
Wholly in your own image. I would change nothing, add or take away,
The same full red flower would model for your mouth—
And from the same seashore
Would I bring the small translucent ear shapes of your ears.
I walk alone, slowly. No hurry. Nobody's waiting.
My love who loved me (she said) is gone. My love is gone.

Shontese Harrell-Ford (Niece)

My Auntie Lindie,

My heart broke in a million pieces when you transitioned. However, I can hear you telling me to mourn now, but don't stay there. I take solace in knowing that you knew just how much I loved and adored you. You made sure your nieces and nephews knew the same.

As a child, I didn't always understand or appreciate your lessons. As I grew older, I realized that you were simply helping to plant seeds. As I look at myself and my sisters, I see a piece of you in each of us. Part of who I am now is because of who you were. I am confident that you were proud of who we grew to become. We became women leaders who are strong, confident, and no-nonsense. We have developed the ability to walk in any situation and command respect, yet remain humble, caring, loving, and family oriented. We are your girls! The seeds you helped plant in each of us have flourished.

So until we meet again, Auntie, I will hold on to all of our memories (especially my favorite green sweater from Macy's) and lessons. I will use what you taught me to inspire our next generation. Your legacy will live on.

With Eternal Love,
Your "Tes"

Shontese Harrell-Ford

Kimberly Harrell-Mills (Niece)

Strong. Honest. Caring. Compassionate. Knowledgeable. Loyal. Lively. Creative. Understanding. Forgiving. Patient. Advocate. Authentic. Joyous. These are just some of the descriptive words that come to mind when I think of my "Aunt Lindie."

All my life, Aunt Lindie has been my cheerleader. Always, you offered words of encouragement, providing great advice, cheering me on, checking me when I was wrong, and celebrating every one of my milestones. I can't think of a time when you didn't show up to celebrate my accomplishments or to just be there when I needed you to be. No matter the circumstance, I could count on you to be there when I needed her. My aunt Lindie!

Aunt Lindie loved me as if I was her own. She had a way of making me feel like I could conquer the world. I remember clearly a time, when I was probably about twelve or so, I spent a weekend with my Aunt Lindie. I loved those sleepover weekends!

One time, we were sitting on her bed having a life discussion, as much of a life discussion as we could between an adult and a twelve-year-old. I remember her encouraging me that day was to be proud of who I was, and that I was pretty in spite of how I felt. She encourage me to not let the words of another person get me down, and to always hold my head high. I remember having so must pride in myself that day. She had that way, an ability to take a person's abilities and turn them into something even greater...she turned me into *something more* that day. My aunt Lindie!

Throughout my life, I have admired my Aunt Lindie for just living as a good human being. Her lively presence, her authentic personality, her forgiving and understanding nature, her joyous outlook on life, and her strength to endure are things that made her amazing. She was such a caring and compassionate person who loved everyone. A true blessing to everyone she encountered. My aunt Lindie!

While I am still trying to wrap my mind around Aunt Lindie no longer being with us physically, I hold on to the wonderful memories. Memories that bring tears to my eyes instantly but accompany a smile to my face. I miss her now and will miss her always, but I do know for certain that she is in heaven, with her pom-poms, continuing to cheer me on for life. My eternal cheerleader... my aunt Lindie!

Earle Jones (Second Husband)

Linda – The Love of My Life and My Best Friend

Linda came into my life by Providence. We were introduced to each other by her childhood classmate, Ron Lewis. Ron and I were good friends in Denver, Colorado. He arranged for Linda and me to meet when I moved back to the Washington, DC area from Denver in 1994. After talking by telephone for a number of weeks, because of her Harvard University Masters' Degree program, Linda and I had our first date just before Christmas in Washington. We had a wonderful evening with dinner and dancing at the old Channel Inn and "The Fox Trap Club." Right away, we learned that we had common interests in family, life, cultural matters, and work.

Linda and I became inseparable. I discovered that Linda was a master "family weaver," connecting the Eatmon, Jones, Harrell, Carroll, and Mitchel families into one large family. She got close to my mother – Sylvia C. Jones –in her final years of life and was my personal rock of support when my

mother passed. She similarly became very close to my father, Earle, Sr. in his final years. I realized early on that I needed Linda in my life as my life partner. We built our dream house in Vienna, VA, got married, and used our home to be the center for our family.

Linda's son, Steve, became my adopted son, and we had an unforgettable time traveling to look at colleges before he set-tled on enrolling at Florida State University. Linda's sister, Jeni, and her brother Jerry both lived with us at different times. But what really stood out were the annual Christmas parties we hosted in Vienna. Linda loved Christmas and her seasonal dec-orations became legendary. When we moved to Vienna, we had two moving vans – one for house furniture and furnishings, and the other for all of her Christmas decorations. Our home was a true "Winter Wonderland."

The Christmas parties were extremely popular. Linda and Steve made skits as a way for attendees to have fun and receive spe-cial gifts as prizes. We also had musical entertainment, portrait painting, clowns, and, of course, Santa for the kids. The parties were family-oriented and fun and became popular for family, church and family friends and work colleagues.

I loved how Linda decorated our home. The landscaping became the envy of our neighborhood and Linda never tired of re-deco-rating the inside of our home. She always had boundless energy that she poured into anything she did. Her professional career was distinguished but her real focus in life was family, church, and community. Linda was an incredible event planner and she helped many friends and family members with planning weddings, anniversary celebrations, birthday and retirement parties. I learned so much about family, friendships, service, and church from having such a smart and talented spouse.

Linda gave me the gift of a lifetime when she planned a special surprise party for me after she'd finished writing and publishing "Touchstone," a book about my family and personal church, school mates and work colleagues who influenced me. She was able to pull this off without my knowing about

and more than 100 people attended the surprise reception. The book itself won the 23rd Annual Colorado Independent Publishers Association Merit Award in the Biography category in 2017.

Linda's love for family made her the matriarch of our extended family. Nothing in the world meant more to her than our grandchildren, Ryan and Rachael. Our Vienna home was specially decorated for them to love. My sister Sylvia Turrell's children and grandchildren became our French family. Steve, Heather, Ryan, Racheal, Linda, and I traveled to France every other year to visit Sylvia, Yvonne, Laurent, Paul, Alexander, Sam, and their family. And the opposite years, the French family traveled to the U.S., staying in our Vienna home to visit friends and family on this side of the Atlantic Ocean. We always spent at least one week visiting Atlantic Coast beaches in Cape May, NJ, or Rehoboth and Bethany beaches in Delaware. Linda also got me involved with helping the planning of family reunions for the Mitchell and Harrell families. And of course, Steve, Linda, and I loved attending the annual "Aunt Ida" July 4th party reunions in Norfolk, VA.

More than anything, Linda was my best friend. I loved the daily conversations we had about everything – family, church, culture, politics, finance and business, and life in general.

Her health was not a subject she shared publicly, but she was courageous in fighting cancer for many years. She always took on the role of being an advisor and caretaker of others, including me when I was diagnosed with prostate cancer. She took care of her mother, Viola Holoman, and her sisters and brothers through a variety of illnesses. She was always a rock of support.

Linda's courage also pushed her to become an award-winning author late in her life and, as part of her Touchstone series, Linda published blogs that provided counsel for self-empowerment. I am proud and honored to have such a talented and Christian wife – Linda Eatmon Jones. She was indeed the love of my life and my best friend.

James Mitchell (Cousin: Mitchell-Newsome)
A Phenomenal Woman

Linda and I have known each other since elementary school. We grew up in the great metropolis of Ahoskie, N.C. I have always viewed her as very smart, driven, perfectionist, athletic, funny, and fun-loving. Only later in life did I find out that we were cousins. In fact, she was the one who told me. I was quite pleased to know that, as she was already quite a role model for our family. After graduating from high school, I moved away to college and never really lived in Ahoskie again. I would visit periodically and might see her if she was in town.

I recall her being the driving force behind the coordination of the Newsome/Mitchell family reunion every two years. That was when we would have the opportunity to talk and catch up with what was going on in our lives. She, Dr. Harold Mitchell, Gloria Parker, and Jewell Wiggins did an outstanding job bringing these two families together. If you made a commitment to Linda, she was going to make sure you followed through.

A little over a year ago, I received a call from Linda, and I was pleasantly pleased, as we had not talked in a while. She informed me that she wanted to write a book about my life and work in the Black Belt of Alabama. After being very surprised, I asked her, "Why would you want to do that? There are a million people with stories like mine." Her response was, "That may be true, but let me write the story." As they say, the rest is history. The book, entitled, "A Touchstone of Determination True Grit: The James Mitchell Story" was released on November 6, 2019.

Linda and I became very close over the last two years and I truly cherished our phone calls, emails, and text messages. Because of her positive energy, she has motivated me to do even more and reach higher heights. In one of our last texts, she was talking about all she had been doing relative to her mother's illness, as well as her own health challenges. I simply said to her that when you have done all you can do, then just stand. She still stands today and forever.

James M. Mitchell

Priscilla Mitchell
(Cousin in-Law: Mitchell-Newsome, Spouse of James)

I met Linda in 2010 and watched her from a distance during the Mitchell-Newsome family gatherings. She seemed to really enjoy herself around family and made every effort to embrace everyone.

The past few years, I would communicate with her via email, mostly sharing information about my husband, James. I remember her asking the family to share stories and achievements of family members to be published in the family newsletter, The Gazette. Sometimes I would think to myself that she was probably tired of me sending her stuff. However, I continued.

In 2018, Linda approached James about writing a book about him. Of course, this came out of nowhere and James was surprised, to say the least. In January of 2019, Linda came to visit us in Alabama. She spent a lot of time shadowing James and interviewing people in Selma and Montgomery. She shared our anniversary, went to a WCCS Lady Patriot basketball game, and a luncheon where gold sponsors from a fundraising event had lunch with James and me. It was during this time that I got to know her.

Later that same year, Linda came back to Alabama. By this time, the book had been completed and we had scheduled our first book signing. It was beautiful. We held it in the Media Room on campus. It was well attended by faculty, staff, students, and members from the community.

We saw Linda again in Clinton, NC, on December 27, 2019, for our second book signing. She and Earle drove down and we had another successful event in the Fellowship Hall at First Baptist Church of Clinton. Some of James's former co-workers from Sampson Community College, family, and friends stopped by to share in the event and to purchase books. Afterward, we got together at our Clinton home and from there went out to dinner.

The last time I saw Linda was in Ahoskie, NC, on January 18, 2020. As always, I was glad to see her. I loved the set up at the book signing. She always put so much love in everything she touched. I loved the stones that she had at the book signings and I always took some home with me. I am so glad I did because now I have reminders of her everywhere! I also have photos of her that will serve as memory keepers.

Her kindness and smile will go on with me. Oh, did I mention she was smart? She teased me about running for mayor of Selma 😊😊😊 I told her that would never happen. Well, I could go on and on, but I will stop here and just say she was once, twice, three times a lady. I am so glad God placed her in my life for a season. Rest In peace, my friend....I love you, but God loves you best.

Priscilla Mitchell
Selma, Alabama

Gloria Parker (Cousin: Mitchell-Newsome)

Linda was a very special person to everyone who knew her. I knew her from high school. Linda and my sister Gwen were very close in school, and so she became a friend of the family. Years later, we found out that not only was Linda a friend, but she also was a close relative.

We were at our first family reunion and Linda was there. I always knew she was a special person but for her to go out of her way to come to our reunion demonstrated just how special she was. That's when I found out Linda was our cousin. I was very happy to see her at our family reunion, and we rekindled our friendship.

Linda accomplished so many incredible things. She had a good head on her shoulders and made a real difference in the world. She was worthy of all the good things that came to her. We were so proud of her. On a scale of one to ten, she was an eleven.

We miss and love you Linda, rest in peace.
Love Dobie (Gloria Parker)

Cheryl Pinkard (Cousin: Mitchell-Newsome)

Linda (a.k.a. my Boo/my Pookie) and I really connected in 2016 when we found ourselves, along with cousin Terri Watts, spearheading the 2017 Mitchell-Newsome Family Reunion. Linda and I worked together like frosting on cake; peaches & cream; harmoniously smooth...a perfect combination! We consistently worked in a judgment-free zone...which was awesome! Linda and I would spend hours on the phone planning, discussing ideas, laughing, and most importantly, getting to know one another on a personal level.

In July of 2017, Linda and I met at cousin Terri's home in Savannah, GA to plan and scout venues for our 2019 family reunion (that wasn't). The three of us had the best time together! It was yet another opportunity to really get to know my cousin Linda...and what an awesome opportunity that turned into.

While in Savannah, I was honored to have been entrusted with some extremely personal aspects of Linda's life. While at cousin Terri's, before we would retreat to our respective bedrooms, we would spend a little time chatting...she could (and did) ask me ANYTHING. She'd say, "Cheryl, I don't know why or how, but I feel extremely comfortable and at ease with you. I feel as though I've known you my entire life." During our nightly chats and many subsequent phone conversations, we both expressed how comfortable we were with one another. Cousin Earle says Linda and I were kindred spirits. Needless to say, Linda, Earle, and I were in agreement.

No one could calm my spirit the way Linda could...she was *sooo* rational, sensible, and compassionate. I really miss that. I really miss her.

I loved chatting with Linda via phone, and when cousin Earle would enter the room...she'd say "Cheryl, your Boo just came in!" Or cousin Earle would say, "Is that my Boo on the other end?"

To most people, that would be nothing more than mere words, but to me, those words meant everything. If Linda and I ever chatted and cousin Earle didn't come onto the scene before our call ended, one of us would say "'Hug my Boo for me" or "I'll hug your Boo for you." We would end nearly every call with *I love you, Boo!* I STILL say that...every night, I say to Linda, "I love you, Boo." Then, I say a prayer of comfort, peace, and provisions for my Eatmon-Jones family.

We never had a conversation without discussing and laughing at something her grandkids, Steve and Heather would say or do. I'm so very grateful for the vids and pics of the grands and recorded links of Steve's sermons. Linda just loved the photo op Steve had with sportscaster James Brown. We discussed that opportunity for a good thirty minutes or so. I really miss those vids, those pics, and those phone-call-sharing moments. While Linda proudly spoke of the grands, Steve and Heather, she was extremely proud of her husband, Earle. I loved the way they complimented each other. Both were busy as bees ALL THE TIME. Reminiscing about those conversations just brought the biggest smile to my face...I pray that I will always have those memories.

On March 20, 2020, Linda and I spoke for nearly two hours. We discussed everything from the books she'd authored to the kids, Steve and Heather, my Earle Boo, future family reunions, our families and her health. As weak as Linda sounded during that conversation, which was my last conversation with her, the one thing that has weighed heavily on my heart, was that she was hurt and confused that a relative she loved, someone who refused to respond to her phone calls and text messages. She was especially hurt by that for two reasons. (1) Family meant everything to her. (2) She didn't understand why or know what she may have said or done to cause such a reaction, or lack thereof. We spoke on that until I reminder her that when someone is angry with you, it's their issue and problem to work through. Especially when you've made multiple attempts to reach out, only to receive silence in return. You've done all you can, the problem is not yours to resolve. Linda said, "You know Boo, you're right...so let's move on to the next topic." The next topic was the family reunion.

If you really knew Linda, you'd know just how much family meant to her. The Mitchell-Newsome Family Reunions; visiting cousin Earle's Sister (and family) in Europe and ensuring Steve and her grands were connected with her mother and siblings meant everything to her.

One of Linda's concerns was that the Mitchell-Newsome Family Reunions would disband. But I assured her that as long as I have breath in me, our reunions would not cease to exist. After making that crystal clear, I could hear the relaxation in Linda's voice.

I'll take our last two-hour phone conversation with me wherever I go. I still hear her laughter during that call, as weak as it was. I still hear "I love you, Boo," which were our last words to each other. Who knew?

Throughout this writing, I originally had referred to Linda in present tense and had many corrections to make...simply because it is still difficult to believe that my cousin, my friend, my Boo, and kindred spirit is no longer with us. But... we are confident, yes, well pleased rather to be absent from the body and to be present with the Lord.

2 Corinthians 5:8 (NKJV)

Linda, I am honored to have been a special part of your circle. Thank you for liking me, loving me, mentoring me, believing in me, trusting me, and confiding in me. I love you and I miss you immensely.

Your kindred spirit,
Cheryl

James and Mary Simmons (Parents of Daughter-in-Law, Heather)

How I met Linda.

One day, a young man I had never seen before came to our door with flowers. His name was Steve. He was to become a very special person to our daughter, Heather. Linda welcomed Heather and was helpful in Steve's courtship of her. Linda welcomed us all. Anyway, this was our first introduction to Linda.

Linda's projects and talents were many. Among others... she excelled at hospitality, event planning, gardening, crafting, outfitting playrooms for grandchildren, remodeling, and working with community organizations.

Overall, in spite of various careers and writing projects, family was central to her. Her love for Steve was so evident–as was her devotion to Earle. Her grandchildren, Ryan and Rachael, were loved, supported, and immensely enjoyed.

Earle's family in France, Sylvia, Yvonne, Laurent, Alex, Paul, and Sam, were very special to her. Special trips and times together with them in the summer were joyful priorities for Linda. The rest of her family was also treasured, and she helped plan large reunions.

Linda had an active career for much of her life, but she was a true homemaker. She had a heart for making her home a welcoming nest for Earle, Steve, and herself as well as extended family and friends.

Her delight in Ryan and Rachael knew no bounds. In Linda's home, they were supplied with loads of toys, stuffed animals, and books – but more importantly, they were given loads of affection and focused attention. She was very concerned with their nurturing and growth. Her faith in Christ was her mainstay, and she loved her church. Linda is a woman, greatly loved, greatly missed, and someone to learn much from, whose legacy lives on.

~Mary Simmons

Corelette Smith (Sister)

God has blessed me to have a sister I can depend on. She has always been a major part of my life and helps me to make wise decisions in my adult life. Even when I didn't realize it, she had my back. She has been there for my family, as long as I can remember.

I now "THANK" God for her. In every major decision, I took her advice. We did not always agree, but she was my *Big Sister.*

I knew she had my best interest at heart. Talking to her sometimes was like she could see the future. I guess that is what wisdom looks like.

I loved my sister and I pray daily to God to give Earle and Steve the strength to carry on. I hope the grandchildren remember how much she loved them. I hope they have fun memories of her. She really loves her family. I know she has made an impact on our life. She always wanted the family to be together. I talked to her before she died; I always want her to be proud of me as I was of her achievement. I appreciated her and wanted her to know I had grown up, become responsible, and was able to make mature decisions. I later realize we were a like in a lot of ways.

I remember when I went to college; I called home and wanted to leave and come back home. Linda said "No!" Well, we know I finished N.C. A&T S.U. and became a teacher. I taught for thirty-two years. That was one of the *best* decisions in the world.

When I got colon cancer, she drove from her house, VA to Ahoskie, NC. and took me to Duke Hospital in Durham. She stayed with me until I got better.

We continued to talk about her and Earle's retirement. I wanted them to enjoy themselves. Life can be so short sometimes.

We continued to plan for my annual trip there to sight-see and visit the family. I think we were both excited about it. This was a pledge I made during the summer, when I got out of school. I cannot thank her enough, but I did. Sometimes we can live a lifetime and not meet people like her. I truly miss my sister. She was my "Angel and Rock."

Corelette H. Smith, Sister

Sylvia Turrell (Daughter-in-Law)

My dearest Linda,

You came into my life like a lifebuoy in a burst of fireworks!

On your arrival to our family, my Dad, Earle Jones, Sr., was very sick and had to be moved from his home. I was on the other side of the ocean, allowed returns to the U.S. only every three to four months. Earle needed a second hand. Then, like a miracle, you were there, doing all the things I wished I could do. All with your *what would become* well-known efficiency and devotion, you were more like a daughter than a daughter-in-law during all that time. I will remain forever grateful to you.

In the following years, you and I continued to become closer as we learned each other. I discovered what a truly lovely woman you were: a woman who was such a very loving and devoted wife to my brother – a truly perfect companion. Through the years, it was obvious that you and I were, in fact, soul-sisters in the important things of life: love of and devotion to those dear to us. I found in you a kind, faithful and loving being, full of smiles and laughter, full of strength and determination.

Family was a sacred thing to you, Linda. From the beginning, you accepted our entire family as your own – accepting us with all our challenges, as well as all of our riches. With a family spanning the Atlantic, you were a true binding force. You were always there – for me, for my grandchildren, and for their parents. And we all knew it. We always knew that you were a person who could be counted on. Your love for Paul, Alex, Sam, Yvonne, and Laurent, your careful inclusion of Naweal – your kind gestures to all of us – all these wonderful characteristics of yours made us look forward to each family get-together. And with your visits here in France, you soon knew all the village, my orchestras, and my neighbors. All the family on the French side adored you. With your interest in their lives and activities, it would be impossible to do anything but love you.

Despite all of your health problems, which you tried to keep hidden away in the background, you continued to give without counting. You freely gave your time, your ideas – yourself. None of that will be forgotten. We will continue to tighten the bond between our respective grandchildren and to keep the Atlantic divide as narrow as possible! You cannot be and will not be forgotten.

So, I bid goodbye to you, my dear *sister*. Please keep your smiling soul close to us all.

With love,
Sylvia

Terri Britt Watts (Cousin: Mitchell-Newsome)
Linda's Impact on Me

I was going through a really rough patch when (my) Mama died. The pain far surpassed anything I've ever experienced in life. Word quickly got around of Mama's passing, and I soon stood engulfed with phone calls rendering condolences. On the day of Mama's funeral, I remember walking into the church ever so slowly. Quietly, I scanned the familiar faces of family and friends, sitting and looking on with broken hearts.

As I sauntered toward the front, I caught a glimpse of an erect posture. Linda Paige sat; she was so beautiful, so strong. Her facial expression exhibited strength, so much so that I felt more energetic after reaching her pew. We made eye contact. Through her eyes, I felt her telling me, "Come on, Terri – Terri," (that's what she used to call me) "You can do this." I shot her a wink. Her posture softened, representing contentment. During the repast, Linda walked up to me and slipped some money into my bra. Only Linda Paige would think of something so humorous, but yet eloquent. It brought a smile to my face. The gesture remained doused with sentimental value as only Linda could convey.

I didn't know her that well and certainly didn't expect to see her at Mama's funeral, but she was there, poised with confidence, assurance radiating. The goal was to help her little cousin through the pain, and she did. From that moment, we grew closer, shared secrets and disappointments.

Linda attended all of the family reunions, exhibiting love for everyone. She studiously took on the chairman's task for our last family reunion, which turned out to be nothing less than sheer success. Her wit and vigor inspired me. It pushed me to view life differently during stressful situations. Linda slipped away too soon. She is undeniably missed, but the beauty of it all, she lives on in our hearts, ...especially in mine.

Terri Britt Watts

Chapter 3

IMPACT AT CHURCH

F aith always played an important part in Linda's life, especially during the last twenty-five years of her life. Growing up in a small town, church is often a staple of the community, especially when it's a small town in the South. She grew up attending Calvary Missionary Baptist Church, where her stepfather, George Harrell, served as a deacon and sang in the choir. She was introduced to the Christianity and professed her faith in Jesus as her Lord and Savior in that same church.

My mother and father attended Little River Church of Christ in Annandale, VA from shortly before the time I was born, until their divorce. Mom taught Sunday school classes there, as I served as her assistant for a few of them, and she volunteered with many of the church events. However, her faith became more solidified and grew deeper when she started attending Antioch Baptist Church in Fairfax Station, VA, in 1996.

She tried out a couple of churches, but she found a home at Antioch when one of her best friends from college, Helen Copeland Latten (who has submitted an essay for this book), invited her, as she was a faithful member at the time. It was there that Linda started becoming more rooted and building deeper longer-lasting relationships with members, deacons, staff, and pastors – many of whom have submitted essays for this section. Attending church there over the years, I was able to see a profound development in character and godliness within her. Those traits served as a foundation for her ability to love so many people, and invigorated the life of impact she would lead. Values were taught from the pulpit –faith in God and love for others, the Bible studies, and the overall interactions with members. All this helped to shift the dynamics of our family and her numerous relationships for the final twenty-five years of her life. Those were the years of her greatest impact.

Her friendships may have been developed in the church, but as you will see in these essays, they transcended the church. The relationships penetrated all areas of life. There was the social: the Christmas parties were populated with people from the church, and the theater group formed where she and Earle, her husband, and many other couples would regularly get together to attend theatrical plays, among many other social outings. The relationships penetrated all the way into the workplace as well, where she and Earle helped someone in the church land a job and even organized his retirement party.

She was not just someone who attended, sat in the pews, and then left. She served and put her heart and soul into the work of the church. She was instrumental in setting up a Young Adult Ministry, providing a retreat/conference for young adults – a difficult group to reach with Christian faith. Through her functions, young adults could have a chance to meet other Christians in their demographic and learn how to apply their Christian faith to their life's situation. She also had a tradition of honoring college graduates with a poster displayed in the church lobby, highlighting their accomplishments and profes-sional aspirations.

Linda was the unofficial Antioch Baptist Church historian as well. She created a document detailing the church's history from its founding until the present day. In addition to her research on church history were her creative displays during Black History Month, since Antioch is a predominantly black church. Her creative displays highlighted historical leaders in the black church community such as Dr. Martin Luther King Jr., Richard Allen, founder of the African Methodist Episcopal (AME) Church, and Rev. Lott Cary, who was considered the first African-American missionary, a man who was influential in the development of Liberia in West Africa.

Antioch is where I came to know Jesus Christ as Lord and Savior as well. Entering high school, I was in the band and played sports such as track and football. My personality embraced trying to be like whoever I was around. I wanted to blend in, fit in, and be accepted. That involved getting into a lot of risky high school behavior, such as partying and drinking. This eventually led me into some trouble.

My mother, of course, was infuriated by what happened. She sent me to meet with the youth pastor of Antioch at the time. I kept the meeting only to oblige her wishes. Also, I knew that playing in the praise band would look good on a college resume and hone my music skills. I was afraid of meeting with anyone in church because of what I had done and become. I was a partier, a kid of worldliness who engaged in "sins." I was a fringe kid who came to church by force and didn't get involved with the youth group. Also, if my family members, who were marginal church-goers, expressed their anger with me for what happened, what more could a holy person say? I knew some people who spoke of going to church and acted differently outside, but a religious person, one whose life was, I thought, holy inside the church walls and outside – how much indignation would he display?

To my surprise, he didn't do that. He showed love, mercy, and compassion, and understanding – that caught my attention. That's not how religious people were characterized in my view. He shared with me the story of David and Bathsheba from 2

Samuel II, how David can still be called a man after God's own heart even after all he'd done. Afterward, I went home to reflect – his example drew me in, but the content of what he taught penetrated me. While he was gracious in his demeanor and showed compassion, he did give stern warnings about the way I was living and the company I was keeping. God, through him, showed me what the gospel and salvation was really all about. Salvation and the Bible became real to me, no longer just independently taught stories, they became my story. God just wasn't just any god, He became my God.

This change in me would not have been possible had it not been for my mother's courageous decision to reach out to the church. Many parents become paralyzed when they have a teenager who is rebellious. Some refuse to reach out for help for fear of exposing their shame or perceived failures as a parent, and many others give up thinking there is nothing they can do and start counting down the days until they leave the house and no longer have to deal with them.

But, Linda trusted this church to help her in time of need. In the years since that time, she has helped so many others in the church. Antioch Bible Church has played an integral part in the development of, not only of my mother, but the entire family.

These are the essays from church:

Rev. Dr. Marshal Ausberry (Senior Pastor)
Phillip Dasher
Eddie Evans
Tiffany Horne
Joshua and Maleka (Matthews) Jackson
Stephanie (Wiggins) Jayaraman
Rev. Melvin Jones (Executive Pastor)
Richard "Spike" Jones
Helen Copeland Latten
Calvin and Veronica Minor

Rev. Bernard Snowden (Discipleship and Teaching Pastor)
Linda Stephens-Jones
Abigail and Curtis Taylor
Laurence Toyer

Rev. Dr. Marshal L. Ausberry (Senior Pastor)

It was a pleasure to serve as pastor to Linda Eatmon Jones. From a pastoral perspective, she hit all the buttons and checked all the boxes. Linda's faith was the driving force in her life. She trusted Jesus Christ and governed her life in obedience to His Word. Linda's faith was so precious to her that she desperately wanted her son, Steven, to be in a relationship with the Lord Jesus Christ.

She prayed many times for her son to be in a relationship with Christ and to be obedient to Christ. There is something about the power of Mother's prayers. God heard her prayers and He more than answered her prayers for Steve.

Linda's faith was also evident in her relationship with her husband, Earle. Linda was a dutiful and loving wife. She was her husband's biggest cheerleader. She was so proud of her husband's accomplishments and while he was too humble to share, she lovingly celebrated Earl's accomplishments.

As a member of Antioch, Linda always showed a deep respect for her pastor. She was always encouraging and, after worship service, she would always give an encouraging word following each sermon. One of the biggest ways Linda blessed me, was that she called me "Her Pastor."

I think for anyone in pastoral ministry, that is one of the biggest and most cherished blessings. When Linda called me her pastor, it was like a thousand blessings in one word. She said it from her heart with such respect and encouragement. It was like one of God's angels telling you to keep on keeping on! I thank God for Linda. She was truly one of God's blessings to all of us!

Phillip Dasher

Mrs. Eatmon-Jones had such an inspiring energy, focus and drive. As a YAM alum, she brought the gift that bounded us together for a common cause–and I think we all remember the group pictures we took as evidence and the impact of her effort. May she rest well.

Eddie Evans
Linda Eatmon Jones, One Warm, Smart and Classy Lady

One of the nicest, sweetest, and most genuine persons that I have ever had the pleasure to meet. Yes, I am talking about Linda Eatmon Jones. So, who is Linda Eatmon Jones and how did we meet each other?

As you can see, I use Linda's full name. I first thought that that was odd, but it makes perfect sense, as I will explain.

I attend Antioch Baptist Church in Fairfax Station, Virginia. Antioch is a church that I have attended since retiring from the military. I have been a member since 1995.

Antioch started out as a very small congregational church that held church services at the Salvation Army on Old Ox Road, near George Mason University. From there, the church moved to Lake Braddock High School to hold its services, but for some reason, my family and I did not follow the church to Lake Braddock High School. Some time later, the church broke ground and built a church at the current location on Little Ox Road. It was at this facility that I first met Linda and Earle Jones.

Every Sunday, my family and I would enter the church facility via the left side of the building. We'd walk down the far aisle and be seated about two-thirds down the pews toward the front. My family and I sat there every Sunday. The Head Deacon was a gregarious and warm-hearted gentleman named, Larry Hester. He named the spot where my family sat, *The Evans Pew.*

As part of the worship service, there was a period to stand and greet your neighbor. It was during this time that I first met Linda. She was a very warm and engaging lady. In fact, I soon noticed that Linda always sat right behind The Evans Pew, especially when Earle was out working with the parking ministry. Linda always had a smile on her face, a word or two, oh well, a few words of encouragement. She would reach out and grab my hand as if you were her long-lost friend, but we had only met recently. I said to my wife, "What a nice person," referring to Linda. Over time, Linda began to engage the Evans family in longer conversations. We found out that Linda and my wife, Patsey, were sorority sisters and they had mutual friends: Abigail Taylor and Helen Latten. Well, that fact merely added another level to the Evans/Jones relationship.

I stated at the onset that I would tell you why it was important for me to use Linda's full name. Well, you probably guessed it, but there was another Linda Stephens Jones at Antioch who just happened to sit on the same side of the church that we did. She was also a member of Delta Sigma Theta Sorority, Inc. That Linda was taller, but equally as nice, and was married to my fraternity brother Richard Spike Jones. So, to differentiate between the two Lindas, I needed to list them in my phone directory with their full name so that I did not get their messages confused.

The real treat came in December when Patsey and I were invited to the Jones' house for their annual Christmas party. Oh, what a treat that was! It was the place to be. All of Linda's immediate family, neighbors, friends, and co-workers were at the party. Linda decorated the house with Christmas accouterments galore.

She had Christmas trees, tinsel, Angels, cerebrums, ribbons, and it seemed like every Christmas decoration imaginable was on display. All of these things were displayed with care and attention to detail. That Christmas Affair was a testament to Linda's character. She was a loving, meticulous and detailed person with a flair for entertaining. The food was equally delicious and plentiful. One might have thought that that was enough. Au Contraire, Linda and Earle organized party games that were very cleverly done and, to top that off, the winners received very nice gifts. Again, Linda's heart for giving was visibly on display. There was no doubt that Christmas was very special to Linda. If you knew Linda, that fact is no surprise because she was a dedicated and committed Christian who loved the Lord. My life was enhanced by the relationship that my family and I developed with this wonderfully talented lady known as Linda Eatmon Jones. I will always remember and cherish my encounters with Linda.

Tiffany Horne

Mrs. Eatmon-Jones truly had an impact at Antioch Baptist Church, but especially with the YAMs ministry. She led the ministry with integrity, influence, and saw the best in all of us. She was not only a teacher and mentor to us, but she was our friend. She always had an activity planned, from Wizard basketball games, picnics, fellowships, and even a retreat. Mrs. Eatmon-Jones did everything with excellence and was very detailed oriented when planning events. She thought of EVERYTHING. Mrs. Eatmon-Jones led us in fun and fellowship but also led us to the Word. She always had a big smile and an encouraging word that led us back to the Christian values she instilled in each of us. Mrs. Eatmon-Jones was truly a Proverbs 31 lady who lived her life fully. She is truly a women of God and we will miss her and her great smile.

Joshua and Maleka (Matthews) Jackson

During our young and professional years, Mrs. Eatmon-Jones, always a pillar, embraced her many roles, one of which was providing great emotional and religious support to both of us. Mrs. Eatmon-Jones organized informal and formal get-togethers that created a ministry for Antioch Baptist Church's young professionals, which ultimately provided fellowship and guidance in our religious growth. In fact, during the years spent in the YAMs ministry, we entered into a courtship that eventually became a marriage.

Today, we reflect on those developmental years. We have realized those wonderful things have happened because of the opportunities, time, and caring religious support given by Mrs. Eatmon-Jones. We are forever thankful to her and the YAMs ministry. Today, Josh and I are happily married with two children and are dedicated educators who use core values to serve our community.

Stephanie (Wiggins) Jayaraman

I will always remember Mrs. Eatmon-Jones' big smile! She was ALWAYS smiling. No matter what was happening, she always wore a smile. Even if you were having a bad day, just seeing that smile would light up a whole room. Her presence and radiating smile was enough to make you feel like you had received a word from God and that He was telling you that everything was going to be fine. Her smile and warmth will truly be missed.

Rev. Melvin Jones (Executive Pastor)

My reflections on the late Sister Linda Eatmon-Jones

I first met Sister Eatmon-Jones when she, Earle, and Steve joined Antioch Baptist Church in 1997. Her unashamed love for God, infectious smile, glowing and bubbly personality, and love for and commitment to her family are a few traits that embedded her into my memory.

Linda was one who took her church membership seriously and became involved in several ministries. As Steve was a young teen when she and her family joined, she became involved in our youth ministry. She not only poured herself into her son Steve, but all youth with whom she came into contact. After Steve grew and matriculated out of youth ministry, Linda remained a person who desired to give back. She became involved in the historical ministry. Her attention to detail, structure, and *class* made this ministry a "perfect fit" for her. She served and served well.

Her devotion to her husband Earle was remarkable. She genuinely loved Brother Earle. I remember when she asked me to write a tribute to him in her book, "Touchstone." She was so excited. She *overemphasized* the importance that this book was to be a surprise for him. When the day came to present it, the event was organized and held with class, a hallmark of how she did things, with class and done right.

God has blessed me to meet many people during my life. Linda is one who made a mark and influence that I will never forget.

To God be the glory!

Rev. Melvin E. Jones, Executive Pastor –
Antioch Baptist Church

Richard "Spike" Jones

A Short Remembrance About Linda Eatmon Jones

To have known Linda Eatmon Jones is both a cherished blessing and a gift from God. I wish that millions more people had known her. For she was truly an example of Jesus living among us.

Linda Eatmon Jones positively and enthusiastically shared her caring, supporting, and sympathetic heart with everyone. I'm sure that it was part of her DNA. No matter whether it was through in-person meets, or by phone, email, text, handwritten letters, or in the award-winning books she authored, these attributes were shared.

One of her greatest attributes that I will mention here is about the way she lifted up the downtrodden, those in need, and those who were pained or suffering. It was done in such a way that it was tantamount to being truly blessed with a healing gift to comfort. I believe, too, that when someone witnessed Linda's gifts for caring and comforting, that witnesser was moved to employ those same attributes with others. I know that I was inspired to do so in my daily walk and journey.

It's obvious that Linda Eatmon Jones truly helped to make us that much better as children of God. In so doing, she showed us great examples of God's desire for us to live together harmoniously and love one another.

Though we will continue to miss her physical presence among us, Linda Eatmon Jones will remain with us in our hearts, minds, and in spirit as long as we're here on this side of glory.

Richard "Spike" Jones

Helen Copeland Latten

A Treasured Friend
"Your life was a blessing
your memory a treasure,
you are loved beyond words
and missed beyond measure."
K. Oliver

Linda and I met on the campus of North Carolina College at Durham, now North Carolina Central University, in the year 1965. Our school's mascot is an eagle, and one can often hear students and alumni say: "The eagle is no ordinary barnyard fowl." Alumna Linda was an extraordinary eagle who achieved renowned success personally and professionally.

While in college, Linda and I pledged to become members of the magnificent, illustrious Delta Sigma Theta Sorority, Inc. After a *challenging* pledge period, we were joyous when we crossed the "burning sands" in December 1967 and became sorority sisters.

In Linda's book, *"Thank You Daddy: 12 Significant Life Lessons,"* she afforded me an opportunity to read and comment on the manuscript before it was submitted to the publisher for printing. This book is about her adoption and the selflessness of her stepfather. As a tribute to Linda and her family, I would like to share:

Thank You, Linda: 12 Lessons You Shared with Us

1. Be Obedient to God's Word
If you love me, keep my commands.
John 14:15

Throughout Linda's life journey that included joys, frustrations, successes, and failures, she lived her life according to God's standards found in the Bible.

2. Show Love
We love, because He first loved us.
1st John 4:19

Linda expressed that it is easy to love those who show love to us. However, there are times that people dislike us for reasons unknown, and we are reminded to show love and wait for the Lord.

3. Be Humble
Humble yourselves before the Lord, and he will lift you up.
James 4:10

Linda was honored by her family and friends because of her humility. She praised others, rather than herself, as exemplified in her first book, which honored her husband, Earle.

4. Have Fun
A cheerful disposition is good for your health.
Proverbs 17:22

If you ever attended Linda and Earle's Christmas parties, you have wonderful memories of fun, well-planned events which included skits, games, and prizes.

5. Give Generously
The generous will themselves be blessed, for they share their food with the poor.
Proverbs 22:9

Linda gave back to the community by serving passionately as the Executive Director for the Fairfax Partnership for Youth program, and as Executive Director for the regional suicide hotline, CrisisLink.

6. Embrace Godly Beauty
Charm is deceptive and beauty is fleeting, but a woman who fears the Lord is to be praised.
Proverbs 31:30

Although well-dressed at all times, Linda paid more attention to her spiritual wardrobe than her earthly outfits. She clothed herself in a wardrobe that reflected gentleness, kindness, and other fruits of the spirit.

7. Respect Others
Do unto others as you would have them do unto you.
Luke 6:31

Linda knew that in honoring others, we follow in the footsteps of Jesus and His love. As such, her circle of friends included individuals from varying socio-economic levels and cultures.

8. Be Trustworthy
Her husband trusts her without reserve and never has reason to regret it.
Proverbs 31:11

From the time Linda and Earle married, they lived a godly life. Linda often spoke about the traits she admired in Earle, and he likewise about her. They truly were soul mates.

9. Practice Good Teaching
Point your kids in the right direction. When they're old, they will not be lost.
Proverbs 22:6

Linda was thankful for Steve, her son, and for two precious grandchildren, Ryan and Rachel, who were blessings from God. She worked hard so that her legacy would be a godly one that would last for generations to come

10. Give Wise Counsel
When she speaks, she has something worthwhile to say.
Proverbs 31:26

Later in life, Linda discovered her love of writing. She poured her heart into sharing information that she felt would be helpful to others, and she succeeded.

11. Remain Faithful
God is a refuge and strength, an ever-present help in trouble.
Psalms 46:1

Linda chose faith over being anxious as the storms of life rolled in and out of her life. She chose peace when circumstances were anything but peaceful.

12. Finish Well
I will extol the Lord at all times; his praise will always be on my lips.
Psalms 34:1

Throughout Linda's time with us on earth, she focused on Jesus and positive experiences. Let us do the same.

Helen Copeland Latten

Calvin and Ronnie Minor
OUR TRIBUTE TO LINDA EATMON-JONES

It was my pleasure to meet this extraordinary young woman, Linda Jones, about twenty years ago at Antioch Baptist Church in Fairfax Station, VA. Linda's smile was contagious and I admired her professional style, abilities to be "on point" about so many things (i.e. , motherhood, womanhood, family values, etc.).

We sparked a true friendship that I will always cherish. With both of us having teenagers who enjoyed their new freedoms, we bonded quickly around many topics while attending youth church activities, e.g., "True Love Waits," Week-end Lock-In, and Annual Women's Retreats/ Conferences. We often continued chatting after church services in the parking lot, on the telephone, having lunch at a nearby restaurant, or having Linda and Earle at our home to just "cool out."

Christmas means LOVE, and no one could share this special holiday with so much love extended to family and friends like Linda and Earle. As you know, Linda never met a stranger; that's just how big her heart was. With Linda's big heart and Earle's joy in making the holiday season bright, these were the specialties they used to transform their home into a true Winter

Wonderland. Together, they immersed us all in the comforts and joy of the Christmas season. As we entered their front door, it was as if we had stepped into a candy store, where all the spectacular Christmas decorations took your breath away! Their home, inside and out, flickered and glittered with the colors of the holiday season. It was quite a beautiful and magical experience! From room to room, tasty hors d'oeuvres, a fabulous selections of foods and sweet desserts awaited us. Their Christmas dinners were scrumptiously delicious!

During the many years of our relationship with Earle and Linda, we were fortunate to develop a bond and passion for the arts, specifically, theater. The group was friends from the church and community, for fifteen years, we supported this activity because of the love and compassion we had for each other and love for the endeavor. The experience was shared by Leroy and Helen Latten, Bob and Iris Warren, Curtis and Abbey Taylor, Hugh and Delores Kelly. We attended events at The Ford Theater, Warner Theater, Kennedy Center, and Arena Stage. Afterward, we dined and shared highlights of the performances. Obviously, we all had opinions as we enjoyed our fellowship planned for future events.

Linda and I shared a special bond for southern hospitality and food. Her love for friends never ceased, I often complimented her on the wonderful spread she and Earle so graciously organized for their annual Christmas party. God put on my heart to do something special for them, for they poured their souls into having family and friends each year celebrate this event in their home. For dinner at our home, I prepared a barbeque feast. Linda raved over the barbecue ribs, which developed into an annual event for us, particularly on her *birthday*. I enjoyed preparing her birthday gift of ribs for her to share with the family. This was my extension of how our family showed love and admiration for her and the spirit and love she conveyed to us.

We were Earle and Linda's guests at many Boule Christmas parties where we always had a good time dancing, taking holiday photos, sharing our projects, and catching up on our grandkids and their latest adventures. At this past Boule Christmas party, we chatted a longer time than usual about life, health, and her accomplishments as a writer. She was very pleased with her recent book award. The book, entitled, "The Dr. James Mitchell Story- True Grit," was a biography about her cousin, James and his impact on the education and economic prosperity in Selma, AL. To our surprise, Linda, always thoughtful, had prepared Christmas gift bags for each guest with a signed copy of this book. As the evening ended, I couldn't believe she was already thinking of a new title for her next book! But then, that was Linda, always the visionary, always inspiring and always a true friend!

"ONE MORE TIME"

Linda, my friend, let me talk to you, let us share one of our stories, just one more time.

Let me see you smile at me, let me hear your laugh; Just because we're friends.

Ignore the tears in my eyes; today, they are more for joy than sadness, JOY, because our Father has released your beautiful soul and set you free from this earthly body which was so heavy to carry in those last weeks of your journey, your kind spirit is NOW, united to HIS in perfect harmony and peace.

HUSH, my friend, my sister, rest and sleep beside the Still Waters you have finally reached after walking through the dark valley, REST, in our Good Shepard's care, until sounds the last trumpet and we will meet again.

This is Ronnie and Calvin telling our friendship story, ONE MORE TIME!

To God Be the Glory,
Calvin and Veronica Minor

Rev. Bernard Snowden, Jr. (Pastor of Discipleship and Teaching)

I came to know Sister Linda as the Young Adult Ministry (YAM's) coordinator at Antioch Baptist Church when I first arrived on staff in December 2001. This ministry was under my leadership as the Director of Youth and Young Adults. Two weeks after I began my position, she hosted a Christmas fellowship at her house for the ministry. When I first entered her home, I remember being amazed by the wonderful decorations displayed. It was as if I were seeing the Macy's New York store at Christmas time.

When I worked with her, I could see her professionalism, planning, and coordinating strengths. I saw her enthusiasm for the ministry and her desire for the spiritual and personal growth of young adults. In fact, the ministry was birthed because of her inquiry and seeing the need for the ministry.

Although she is no longer here with us, I can still see her smile, hear her voice, and the distinct way she pronounced my name. Linda embraced me from the start and was a great encouragement to the young adults she touched and me. I am forever grateful for her friendship, excellent service, and influence in my life.

Rev. Bernard Snowden Jr.
Pastor of Discipleship and Teaching
Antioch Baptist Church

Linda Stephens-Jones
Happy To Be Called Linda Jones, Too!

Linda Eatmon-Jones is one of the many bonuses that came into my life through my marriage to Richard Spike Jones. She and Spike became fast buds where we all worshipped at Antioch Baptist Church. Once they learned they both grew up in North Carolina and attended North Carolina Central University. Those two factors alone set the space for them to become good friends and opened the door for me, to what grew into one of the most inspiring and precious relationships.

I remember making a joke to Linda not long after we became members at Antioch. I told her now there were two Linda Joneses in our church. I wanted her to behave, lest I be mistaken to have done something that she was in fact responsible for. Welp, as I got to spend time with her, I experienced and learned of her tremendous faith, love, generosity, smarts, leadership, and ingenuity. So, it didn't take long for me to do a 180. I let her know I had a change of heart and that I didn't mind after all if people got the two Linda Joneses mixed up. 😊😊

Linda showered her entire circle of friends and me with her warmth and loving presence to such an extent that I sensed we all felt we were her bestie. Spike and I were blessed to not only experience her love first hand, but to witness her sharing her ingenuity and love of family and friends at their Christmas parties and at the Sigma Pi Phi Annual Christmas Ball.

No descriptions are adequate for their joy and love-filled Jones' Christmas parties. We adults reconnected with our carefree, happiest selves and children ran around in glee, all of us wandering through with delight at the room by room detailed decorations, merriment, food, and games. One year, Linda showed me a small photo album she kept of pictures of the different themes used for the parties over the years. Get this, she never used the same theme in sequence. So we were always surprised to see what her ingenuity had come up with when we arrived at the Christmas party!

I had the great honor of interviewing Linda for my radio talk show in 2016, where she shared some powerful life lessons that I'll never forget. I must share a couple here:

I had asked Linda to tell me a bit about her adorable grandchildren, who were seven and five at the time. She shared that when you have grandkids, it's hard to contain your joy and that they are such a blessing. She noted how she enjoys watching over them in such a way that they can be carefree and not worry about anything. Then she dropped this incredible analogy: The way her grandkids never have to worry because they know Grammy is there. It is the same way God is with us. He is looking out for us every moment (like a Grammy with her grandkids) to the point that we don't have to worry or think about our needs. WOW!

When I asked Linda to kind of sum up how it is that she's faced life's greatest challenges and remained steadfast, she said it is by her faith in God and staying grateful, not just for the miraculous big things, but for the small things as well. Linda shared this as her formula: Prayer + Gratitude = Peace.

The last time Linda and I were together was with Spike and me as her and Earle's guests for the 2019 Sigma Phi Pi Christmas Gala. She knew that I was at the early stages of working on a compilation book and asked how things were going. I began to whine about not being a writer and how hard it was to get going with it. I must have expected Linda to join my pity party, but she did not. I clearly remember her telling me that God had given me the idea and equipped me to write the book, so I needed to get on with it. I loved and will always be grateful that Linda gave me some tough love when I had started to doubt myself. Thanks to that discussion with Linda, I am confident that I will get my book completed.

I'm deeply honored to share the name *Linda Jones* with the brilliant, warm, loving, and faith-filled Linda Eatmon-Jones. I'm so thankful that God allowed us to share a season of life together. She enriched my life in more ways than I can put into words. I will never forget the way I was embraced, inspired and loved by Linda Eatmon-Jones.

Linda Stephens-Jones

Abigail and Curtis Taylor

On behalf of the Taylor Family, I would like to extend our deepest sympathy and love to Earle, Steve, Heather, Ryan, Rachel, and to Linda and Earle's entire extended family.

I am so incredibly grateful to have had the opportunity to know Linda as my Sister, my friend, my Delta Soror and, most of all, my sister in Christ. Linda lived an exemplary life full of passion, gratitude and boundless energy. Linda used her gifts in many church ministries at Antioch to include the Church History Committee, Scholarship Committee, and the student ministry for college students. My heart is filled with gratitude to have personally experienced her love and friendship through so many of her kind, thoughtful and generous gestures. Once when I had surgery, Linda came over to my house and sat with me and even fixed my breakfast and lunch.

I still remember how in awe I was over how Linda beautifully decorated the room for my retirement party and for my 40th wedding anniversary celebration. Linda passionately and generously supported her friends. I believe that Christmas might have been one of Linda's favorite holidays and Christmas parties at Linda and Earle's house were always festive events filled with elaborate decorations, games, music, laughter, and fellowship.

Linda's love and devotion to her husband, her son, her daughter-in-law, and her grandchildren are an inspiration and a reminder to me to love my family with all my heart. Linda was her family's best cheerleader and supporter. She was an extraordinarily dedicated grandmother. She frequently babysat her grandchildren, providing them a roomful of books and toys in their own playroom in her home. Even though they lived in Maryland, she traveled to support them in their schools and often served as a classroom volunteer.

I am in admiration of Linda's appreciation of life's journeys of others. She did not just talk about legacies of those she admired the most, she wrote three "Touchstone" books honoring the legacies of Earle, her father, and her cousin. I am tremendously grateful for Linda's personal and powerful legacy that she leaves her family and friends, which will be forever cherished and remembered.

Linda loved flowers, gardening, and landscaping. She diligently and meticulously cared for her gardens as she did the people in her life. Linda's gardens represent the beautiful woman that she was: amazing, authentic, extravagant, creative, unforgettable, unique, graceful, gracious, humble, sweet, playful, and one of a kind.

In closing, I would like to quote an anonymous quote that I believe best sums up the wonderful full life that Linda led:

> "Life is not a journey, to the grave with the intention of arriving safely in one pretty and well-preserved piece, but to slide across the finish line, broadside, thoroughly used up, totally worn out, and loudly proclaim – "WOW – What a Ride!"

Our earthly loss is truly heaven's gain. I will forever miss you, my dear sister.

Abigail and Curtis Taylor

Laurence Toyer

Mrs. Linda Eatmon-Jones was always so encouraging to those of us that were part of the YAMs group. She always had a smile on her face and I could tell that she truly enjoyed leading the group. She had a passion that was genuine. During the early college years, we were faced with situations that we had not experienced before, but Mrs. Eatmon-Jones was always there to give good Christian-based guidance. Even years after I moved away from the area, I would recall topics that we discussed and the kindness that she always displayed towards me and the others in the group.

Chapter 4

WORK LIFE

L inda's career was one that defies the odds – born to parents who never married and growing up as a black woman in North Carolina during the Jim Crow segregation where you are already at a disadvantage for opportunities, resources, social networks, and admissions into top-tier institutions. It would have been easy to rely on various built-in excuses to explain the lack of socio-economic and career success, and few would have expressed any dissent. But this is Linda Eatmon-Jones, and she refused to let her life be defined by pity.

Her career can best be defined by a lifelong process of hard work, continual learning, and taking on new challenges. She was a lifelong learner and never saw herself as too old to try new things or learn new skills. Whenever, she was met with a challenge, she rose to meet it head-on, rather than try to avoid it or settle for something less.

Linda worked hard throughout high school, achieving straight As throughout. That earned her acceptance to North Carolina Central University in Durham, NC, a very sought-after Historically Black College and University (HBCU) at the time, where she double majored in math and psychology. Her career began in 1969 in Northern VA. The field of computer programming as mainframe computers were becoming more and more popular. She described herself as "one of those nerdies," and her career led her to a position with more responsibility at Pension Benefit Guaranty Corporation (PBGC) in the late 1970s, developing actuarial and financial models in the secondary market. In 1988, she was offered a coveted management position in the same field at the Federal National Mortgage Association, known to the general public as Fannie Mae.

Being in technology for a while, she wanted to improve her people skills. She left her secure career in technology in Northern Virginia, moved to Boston, Massachusetts for a while to go back to school, and worked extremely hard to get a master's degree in a short amount of time from Harvard University in Business Administration in 1994. The Harvard degree opened up avenues for advancement into management, and her ascension up the corporate ladder sped up significantly. One of her crowning achievements was helping her employer at the time – Fannie Mae – get through the Y2K crisis. Her leadership – as you will see in the essays – was evident in helping her company avoid all of the potential pitfalls.

However, being in corporate America did not give her the time that she felt she needed to properly give back to society. I'm not saying that one can't do this while working in corporate America, but for Linda, her burden was great and she wanted to do all she could. For her, that meant leaving corporate America to work in the non-profit sector. That began with her degree from George Mason in 2005 in Organizational Development. Again, leaving a secure career at Fannie Mae, where she worked in Business Administration, she took the risk to improve herself and invest in others.

Her tour through the non-profit sector spanned over a decade and involved stints running six tax centers at DC Cash. The centers provided assistance in filing taxes for those in underprivileged areas of downtown DC, Fairfax Partnership for Youth: an organization for at-risk youth, Crisis Link: a suicide prevention hotline and Child Help: serving on the board of an organization dedicated to fighting against child abuse. She combined her skills developed in her first two phases of life, finance and business administration, to provide steady management and fundraising on the weekends to help them survive and carry out their mission.

Hard work, continual learning and taking on new challenges – the hallmark of any successful career, and definitely one that has impact on others. Her work ethic was unmatched by anyone. Two major career shifts require a lot of hard work that many people are not willing to undertake. Even for non-work-related projects, such as the annual family Christmas party, she threw herself into it 100 percent, working day and night to see it through to success. At work, as you notice in the essays, it was the same theme. Throughout these essays, you will see testimonials of not only her work-ethic but a wonderfully woven together masterpiece of career skills – technical competencies, management, collaboration, educated risk-taking balanced with a commitment to timeless principles, and most of all, a willingness to serve and put others first.

Here are the essays representing her impact in the workplace

Awilda Gunderson-Ortiz
Colonel Winston M. Haythe (Ret.)
Edward Moawad, Esquire
Jamie Mueller
Carol Teasley
Rich Valus

Awilda Ortiz-Gunderson

It was 2010 when I first met Linda. I interviewed with her at Crisislink. Linda was the Executive Director of the organization and she hired me as her Call Center Director. Linda and I hit it off immediately. Her personality and positive attitude brought joy to everyone around her. During my first two days, Linda scheduled an interview for the local paper; she wanted the community to learn more about my experience and the skillsets I was bringing to the CL. I was extremely impressed by her willingness to share the spotlight. No other boss had ever done that for me. Everyone loved and respected Linda not because she was the *Boss Lady* but because how well she treated everyone around her. Linda was an instant magnet for people.

Through our time at Crisislink, Linda and I encountered a lot of difficulties with some of the CL board members. There were times where I wanted to quit because it was so difficult to manage all the

different personalities and egos of most of the board members. Linda always supported me and stood by my side. She encouraged me not to give up and showed me how to rise above those people who only

purpose in life is to gain for themselves and not value or respect others opinion or hard work.

Needless to say, both Linda and I left CrisisLink. After our departure, the organization fell to ground within two years. They lost all the funding and donors that we'd brought to the organization. And so, CL existed no more. They had to join forces with another crisis organization that took over and acquire CL call center and services.

Linda and I became very good friends. She was not only my boss but also a mentor and spiritual guide. We had great moments together. We used to meet for lunch at least once a month when I lived in VA and, of course, attended many Christmas parties as well as baptism and birthday parties of her precious grandchildren. She is phenomenal at coordinating party she was the best at everything she did.

I learned so much from Linda, not only on the professional front but in personal life as well. Linda showed me that being firm and having character did not have to come with disrespect for others. On the contrary, "Be firm, Awilda, but remember to always be humbled" was her mantra for me. As a young woman, I wasn't blessed with the patience and wisdom that Linda possessed, but through the ten years of friendship with Linda, she taught me how to be humbled and patient and always look at the bright side of things. I lost my mother when I was eighteen years old and Linda took me under her wing and made me a better professional, a better parent, and overall, a better person. Through Linda, I learned by her interactions with people and the way she treated everyone around her with kindness, respect, humility, but overall, with love.

Thank you, Linda, for being a great role model for me, for teaching me patience, humbleness, kindness, trust for our greatest God and the plan He had for us, for everything you taught me, I will forever be grateful.

I will forever cherish and remember you as the great woman who inspired me to be the best version of myself that I could be. Until we meet again in heaven, I am sure you will be the angel guiding us to the angel's dance.

Forever in my Memory, Linda
Awilda C Gunderson (Ortiz)

Colonel Winston M. Haythe (Ret.)

TITLE
"Lady Bountiful" of Time-Honored Standards, Beliefs and Traditions

INTRODUCTION
Linda Eatmon-Jones was truly a modern-day Lady Bountiful who was widely known for her exceptional kindness, diverse talents, and generosity toward one and all. Yet, unlike the fictional character Lady Bountiful in dramatist George Farquhar's 1707 play The Beaux' Strategem, Linda made everyone feel like her own best friend and equal. To know her was to love her!

YOUR EXPERIENCE/SITUATION/COMMENTS
My initial meeting with Linda did not go according to plan—but that's a very good thing. She and I met the first time over lunch in the early spring of 2010 at the Cosmos Club in Washington, DC at the suggestion of a local psychiatrist who was acquainted with each of us. At that time, Linda was the Executive Director of CrisisLink, a nonprofit organization in suburban Washington that focused on suicide prevention counseling; an entity began forty years prior. It was initially known as the Northern Virginia Hotline. At the time of our luncheon, I had relatively recently experienced the agonizing loss of my own adult son.

Why our initial meeting did not go according to plan was because each of us, I am confident, had

allotted approximately one hour on our busy calendars for this luncheon. Yet, when we left the club some 3-1/2 hours later, we did so as "new best friends for life" who had so very much in common. That highly successful first meeting where we "just clicked" ultimately led to my appointment to the CrisisLink Board of Directors a few months thereafter.

On October 27, 2010, Linda presided over CrisisLink's Inaugural Fall Forum, a black-tie event held at the Cosmos Club for fifty dinner guests to raise awareness of suicide in the Washington community and the acute need for financial support. As the keynote speaker for this glittering evening, Linda had selected U.S. Army Major General Mark Graham, who, along with his wife Carol, had become tireless champions of military and civilian efforts to promote mental health and suicide-prevention awareness and to eliminate the stigma surrounding mental healthcare. General and Mrs. Graham had adopted this cause to honor the memory of their two sons, Second Lieutenant Jeff Graham, who was killed by an improvised explosive device (IED) weapon in Iraq in February 2004, and their son Kevin, a Senior Army ROTC Cadet, who died by suicide in June 2003, while studying to become an Army doctor at the University of Kentucky.

That one spectacular evening for suicide awareness, as carefully envisioned and planned in infinite detail by Linda, with full backing and support by the CrisisLink Board of Directors, helped to elevate a once relatively obscure, local operation in a suburb into a nationally spotlighted organization on suicide awareness and prevention in Metropolitan Washington, DC. Capitalizing on the overwhelming success and favorable publicity generated for CrisisLink by that Inaugural Fall Forum at the Cosmos Club on Embassy Row in 2010, Linda again relied on her visionary talents and finely-honed instincts in planning the annual fundraiser for CrisisLink in the spring of 2011. First, instead of holding the event at a non-descript ballroom in Arlington County, Virginia, as in prior years, Linda chose the beautiful, historic landmark of the Carnegie Institution for Science as the location for the CrisisLink fundraising extravaganza.

That institution's grand neoclassical Sixteenth Street façade lends to the grandeur of one of the most prominent thoroughfares in Washington. Nestled between Dupont Circle and

Logan Circle in the heart of the city, this highly prestigious location bespeaks of forward thinking and planning, as well as discoveries for the betterment of humankind. As guests arrived that lovely spring evening, they were bedazzled by the majestic setting, lovely decorations, the libation offerings, and the food locations. There were also the numerous items provided for silent auction, as well as a live auction in the auditorium directed by a professional auctioneer. All highly desirable auction items had been donated by supporters of CrisisLink.

Most striking of all in setting the tone for refined elegance for the evening was Linda herself: She came attired in a stunningly beautiful spring suit in the exact colors of bright green and white of the CrisisLink logo, with matching accessories. Linda's outfit alone was a shining example of the careful planning that she had adopted for this event. Fashion designer Coco Chanel would have been envious of Linda's sheer elegance and style that evening.

At the conclusion of that extraordinarily unprecedented evening, after final receipts had been tabulated, Linda's CrisisLink fundraising event for 2011 had quadrupled the total amount of donations over what was raised the previous year. She was indeed "Lady Bountiful" who delivered with results where it mattered most; namely, in the acquisition of resources for a worthy cause.

After breathing new life and energy into CrisisLink, Linda eventually felt led to provide a helping hand to another local charity that was not focused on suicide awareness and prevention but one with a broader base of community need. For this, she chose the Koinania Foundation, Inc., which is a community of sharing founded in the 1960s in nationally prominent Fairfax County, Virginia. Koinania is a Christian organization with the capacity to provide a way for local churches to combine their resources to more efficiently and effectively provide emergency services and compassionate care to people in the local community.

Once again, Linda, with her inimitable determination, turned to her friends and other influential individuals within the local community to acquaint them with the important work that Koinania was undertaking and to ask for their support. When Linda came calling, no one could resist her contagious enthusiasm and compelling drive. They pulled out their checkbooks and responded generously to her polite but tactfully firm requests. Once again, Linda delivered the goods! Notwithstanding her highly visible, ever-demanding professional positions, Linda always kept her eye on the ball of her own academic development and growth. During her career path, Linda also acquired graduate degrees at both George Mason and Harvard Universities. In addition, she found time to write and publish three books, each of which has been a literary success.

Finally, no reflection on Linda's exemplary life could ever be complete without mention of her skills as a hostess within her home and in particular her legendary Christmas parties. Movie producer Cecil B. DeMille, who was known for his extravagant productions such as The Ten Commandments, could not possibly have produced a script to rival Linda's elaborate plans for her annual December event. As Linda's husband Earle would know, I can envision that literally weeks were devoted to decorating their large home from basement to attic for the grand soiree.

Invitations to those occasions were the talk of the town even before they arrived, shortly after Thanksgiving Day to the privileged recipients. I suspect that I was typical in the fact that I would not dare to accept an invitation to another Saturday social event during the month of December until I had first received and responded to Linda's lovely invitation. Her legendary party each year was simply an occasion not to be missed. No exceptions—no excuses!

Back in her day, Perle Reid Mesta, Washington socialite and political hostess as well as United States Ambassador to Luxembourg in 1949-53, was known as "The Hostess with the Mostess." While I was too young to have attended one of Ms. Mesta's parties, I simply cannot imagine that her events could possibly have outdone Linda's annual festive offering. Linda "officially opened the Holiday Season" for so many of us. Her grand parties will forever be missed by one and all.

In summary, Linda Eatmon-Jones was a true gift of God's great blessing to the world. She was a well-educated, acutely-focused woman of infinite, boundless energy and substance, who always brought meaning and determination to the task at hand. She also graced the world around her with such finesse, beauty, and utter charm. She was never frivolous or too relaxed, and she relieved so much pain and suffering for so many. Unlike so many other professionals in the nation's capital and elsewhere, Linda never sought personal attention or self-aggrandizement. Thus, she did not retain a public relations firm to promote her credentials and accomplishments.

Her actions of charity, benevolence, and generosity—coupled with her grace, wit, and charm—will live on in perpetuity in the minds and hearts of those of us who were privileged enough to have known her. Linda was truly a modern-day Lady Bountiful, who will be remembered forevermore!

WINSTON M. HAYTHE
Colonel, U.S. Army (Retired)
Professor and Counselor at Law
Washington, DC, July 4, 2020

Edward Moawad, Esquire

There are those we meet, and we forget the instance! And those who we meet; we are saddened by their departure.

It is like they have never left. They stay with us all. There's not a time when you don't hear their voice! "You should see this!" "Look this way and the light will appear!" "Liars are blind to the next step!" "God is just!" And more....but it's their remarkable unshakable trust in God, even when it looks to the blind that God might not have been just!

Lucky are those who are never forgotten. They touched our souls, etched our memories and shone a light in our lives and made sure they kept the candle sparkling long after they are gone; its wax never vanishes. Miraculous.

Fortunate we are to have met them as well; rich are the ones who could count more than one in their lives! And we are the lucky souls that we have lived in their sphere.

You haven't left, my dear sister. Your light shines eternal. Happy, sad, or in crisis, your voice whispers, loudly, you are here to light the way.

Linda lived for others. It's always been this way. Remarkably more so, each felt as if they are the only ones that mattered in her life at those moments. No exceptions. Linda was that thankful, grateful soul that knew that she was given a-plenty, and she has to give as much of what she was given while she can, while she was here physically.

We shall meet again. It's our fortune if we meet you again. Where you are now, I could only imagine how many souls you are leading!

> "You mustn't be afraid of death
> you're a deathless soul
> you can't be kept in a dark grave
> you're filled with God's glow."

Jamie Mueller

I had the pleasure of working with Linda at CrisisLink around 2009. It was a time of growth for

the organization but also, as with all nonprofits during the recession, a time of incredible stress and worry. Linda faced the challenges we faced as, I would assume, she met all of life's challenges – with optimism, confidence, and strength.

CrisisLink's mission was to be there when people needed someone to answer. We were combating a horrible climate of poor mental health, rising military suicide rates, and an increased need for safety-net services. It was an innovative organization with incredible volunteers and staff. We were proud of ourselves. Our organization was considered a leader in suicide prevention and training throughout the United States. At the time when Linda was at the helm, we were expanding 2-1-1 VIRGINIA operations, taking on new grant projects, and beginning to support local survivors of suicide in the immediate aftermath of a tragedy. We had a lot on our plate but Linda managed it all with grace and ease.

CrisisLink also moving its operations, along with 100 volunteers, to new office space, which

required extreme coordination and resourcefulness. Linda put her faith in my ability to project manage the office move, which was a big responsibility for a young professional. I learned a great deal from her during this time. She taught me a lot about looking outside the box, being resourceful, finding work-arounds, and doing my due diligence. She held me responsible for my actions, which, surprisingly, is something many managers don't do. She never let me slide past a mistake. I learned more in my time working for her than with any other manager before her because she put full trust in me and held me to account for my actions.

Being an Executive Director of a nonprofit is one of the hardest, and sometimes, thankless jobs

a person can hold. It can also be one of the loneliest jobs. You are being scrutinized by your staff and your board. Linda never let us feel her worry, isolation, or doubt (if she had any). She led with humor, a smile, and optimism that carried us through some rough patches. I will remember Linda as a strong and confident leader who knew how to tell a story. She always had a story to tell about her childhood, her family, or her hometown. I feel lucky to have known Linda and to have worked for her. It pains me to know that there will be folks out there who don't get to experience her stories, leadership, and wisdom.

However, I know the lessons I learned from her still impact how I go about my work today and will trickle down to those I manage and work with. I also know that she was an incredible mother and wife, and her memory and lessons will shine through her family for generations to come.

God bless you, Linda, and may you rest in eternal peace. Much love to you and your family.

Jamie Mueller

Carol Teasley

Remembering Linda Eatmon Jones – from Carol Teasley

Let me say that Linda Eatmon Jones was one of the most generous, caring, and selfless people I have ever known. She was beautiful inside and out. I had the pleasure of meeting Linda during my very first introduction to my new colleagues at Fannie Mae in February of 1993. It is always interesting to be the new kid on the block and to see who steps up to help you learn the ropes. For me, that person was Linda – she was the first to introduce herself and she sat next to me during the meeting to explain things that might not be readily evident to a newcomer. I have never forgotten her kindness that day.

During my nine years at Fannie Mae, Linda came to work for me when I was assigned the three-year project to coordinate our Year 2000 (Y2K) preparations corporate-wide. Linda was my organizational go-to person for three years. Linda had strengths that complimented my weaknesses. Her attention to detail and gentle approach to dealing with people were extraordinary and certainly saved me many times. During the work on Y2K Linda coordinated my materials for Board of Directors meetings, regulatory meetings, and internal departmental updates – and she made me look so good!

One of Linda's most important responsibilities was the creation and organization of a monthly gathering of Washington area professionals responsible for a Year 2000 activity. Linda was responsible for ensuring we had our speakers lined up in addition to all of the meeting logistics and participant communication. The group grew from an anticipated 75-100 initially invited people to over 350 regular attendees. She was well known throughout the Y2K community and became a contact person for questions regarding our activities at Fannie Mae. To me, she was just amazing in her ability to pull off these packed-house meetings without a hitch.

The culmination of the Year 2000 project was at midnight on December 31, 1999, when we all held our breath as the year rolled over into 2000. The timing required that no key person at Fannie Mae could enjoy the biggest New Year's Eve celebration of their lifetime, so it fell to Linda to plan a "bash" that our employees and their families could enjoy together. Linda's New Year's Rocking Eve rivaled anything you could have seen in Times Square. Husbands, wives and children of all ages had a wonderful time in an atmosphere of celebration and togetherness before our real work began in the late evening. Truth be told, it was Linda's job to make sure that all essential staff were accounted for and completely sober!

The last time we met was for lunch somewhere near Chantilly and we both caught up on what we were doing. I was thrilled to find out that Linda had begun to write and had become an award-winning author. I am so happy to have been a part of her life and happy that she was part of mine. I will forever remember the honor of attending her beautiful wedding to Earle and enjoying a reception full of joy and happiness for the newlyweds. I am sure she is in heaven now and chairing the welcome committee.

Rich Valus

After nearly thirty years, I still can vividly remember my first meeting with Linda. May 1990, it was for a project manager job with Fannie Mae in Washington DC. She made a lasting impression on me as she is the one person that I still remember chatting with that day (besides sharing a cab back to the airport with a couple of Nolan, Norton consultants) that made the decision to take the job easier. What made that interview memorable was the tone of our conversation – inviting, light, warm and personable. Linda's characteristics that stayed true for the next fifteen years that I was at Fannie. I also remember her presence – Her sense of humor, her smile, her eyes, her hair and how tall she was.

Although I never worked directly for Linda, we worked together on projects, most notably Fannie Mae's preparing for the infamous Y2K event. It was during this project that I got to know her better, working alongside her throughout the project. Her wit and sense of humor took the day to day doldrums out of multi-year project that at times felt like we were herding cats. It was during this time at a number of meetings that I witnessed her way of managing hard conversations with our peers with her demeanor, sense of humor and wit. We all learned a lot about each other during that project and I learned a lot from her and the other members of the Y2K team that I still leverage to this day. That includes manage with humility; we all succeed–or I have failed; your team is only as strong as the weakest member.

Probably the one thing that she imprinted on me the most was the importance of family–everything else is a distant second.

Chapter 5

FRIENDS AND COLLEAGUES

To say that Linda was a social person is a tremendous understatement. Linda was the life of the party and a social but-
terfly from her youth all the way to her last years. Making a
separate chapter for friends almost seems redundant because
to her, friends were family – she treated them the same way.

There were many ways in which Linda cultivated relationships with friends. She and Earle were part of a *theater group*
made up of a handful of couples within her church. The group
derived its name from various social outings going to see various plays. There was a charitable club she was a part of in the
1980s. There were always various cookouts and social outings
at the house, which were always filled with people who came
from near and far. But the biggest one of them all were the
annual Christmas parties, which sometimes would have up to
100 in attendance, people from all aspects of life, neighbors,
work, community organizations and the like.

When I think about how she approached her friendships, I am
reminded of chapter 2 of the book of James from the Bible. In
this chapter, James reproves his audience for showing favor-
itism among certain people in the church, namely those who
are rich, and showing contempt to those who are poor. Look

at the piercing perspicacity of his words in the first four verses of this chapter:

> *My brothers and sisters, believers in our glorious Lord Jesus Christ must not show favoritism. Suppose a man comes into your meeting wearing a gold ring and fine clothes, and a poor man in filthy old clothes also comes in. If you show special attention to the man wearing fine clothes and say, "Here's a good seat for you," but say to the poor man, "You stand there" or "Sit on the floor by my feet," have you not discriminated among yourselves and become judges with evil thoughts? (James 2:1-4, New International Version)*

Linda found friends in unlikely places and it seemed like everyone she came in contact with had value and had a significant place in her life. The Christmas parties had a diverse attendance from contractors who came to do work on the house. I met the contractors, got to know them and their families as well. There were the people who would come to fix refrigerators, air conditioners, and remove wasp nests felt like family. I remember her taking one of them under her wing and spending time giving him business advice and using her Harvard degree to help set him up for financial success.

Many people in situations like hers, being successful in business and living in upper middle class neighborhoods, can often look down on contractors and people who do similar jobs. The way in which many of these types of people communicate with them can appear dismissive, but to her they were like family and the way in which she communicated with them, and joked around with them attested to that. She treated them the same way she treated the fellow board members who were financially wealthy and very decorated businessmen and women.

The Christmas parties, where one would find her most com-plete collection of friends, featured a mosaic of diversity. People from all types of socio-economic classes, racial and ethnic backgrounds, religious backgrounds, age groups and career paths came together and bonded. There were no unre-solved conflicts, no heated verbal exchanges, no altercations, just a heavy dose of love being expressed. That was Linda, she was able to communicate with and build relationships with so many different types of people with ease. For her, friend-ships crossed the boundaries that many people these days are afraid to cross.

When I got married, I presented to her a potential seating chart for the guests. Being ethnically mixed and marrying into a Caucasian family meant that there would be guests from dif-ferent backgrounds. My original idea was to have people sit with those they were comfortable with, since they would be more apt to conversation and feel at ease during the reception. Her reaction, however, was not one of satisfaction. Why? The tables were all segregated, blacks were sitting with blacks, and whites were sitting with whites. Her suggestion? Mix them up, allow people to get a little uncomfortable, but over time they will build new relationships, broaden their horizons and learn something new. That's the way she thought and that's why her collection of friends were so diverse.

These essays come from an array of different backgrounds, but they all speak to the same theme: someone who loved with all she had, someone who treated everyone like family, and someone who was no respecter of persons, whether rich, poor, black, white, tall, short, younger or older.

The essays from friends are as follows:

Rev. Hugo Cheng
Mary Goldwag
Liana Leiprichakul

Bob and Diane Nock
Carlos Palacios
Manya Raynor
Joshua Rich
Cynthia Robbins
The Shiu Family
Charisse Tang

Rev. Hugo Cheng
My Memory of Linda Paige Eatmon Jones

By Hugo Cheng

Of all the people who will write about Ms. Eatmon Jones, (and from what I do know about her, I am pretty certain that if she read this first line, she would tilt her head, look directly at me in the eye, with a smile, but a firmness in her voice, and say, "Now you know you should call me Linda and not that formal of a title!" and she would give me a hug), I may be the one who knew her for the shortest amount of time and knew her the least, so I may not have as much to say as others. But I still felt compelled to write this down in honor of her, because even for the short amount of time that I knew her, she made a great impression on me and it was a blessing to know her.

The first time I met Linda was when I just started to serve at the Chinese Bible Church of Maryland as the new senior pastor in the fall of 2016. I saw a well-dressed lady busy running around by herself in our fellowship hall. She was decorating our fellowship hall with a wonderful fall theme (after that, each fall I see our fellowship hall all decked out in a wonderful fashion, I know Linda has been there with her creative, joyful, and servant's touch). So I went to say *hi* to her and introduce myself, and she in turn introduced herself to me in a very friendly manner. She stopped what she was busily doing to take the time to chat with me. There are some people that even when you just met them for the first time, you can sense that they are full of joy, life, and energy. Like a good glass of wine (or good coffee, tea, juice, whatever you prefer), or an amazing pot of stew, filled to the top, brimming over with goodness and wonderful flavor, Linda gave off that impression right away. Some words I can come up with to describe immediately are: vibrant, joyful, determined, confident, kind, friendly, and creative. When I spend time to chat with her, I always walk away feeling energized and blessed.

Another way I have been blessed indirectly by Linda is through her son, Rev. Steve Eatmon. He and I serve together at CBCM on the pastoral staff team, and I am sure that Linda was used by God in many wonderful ways to form and shape Rev. Eatmon to become the godly, faithful, helpful, skillful, and friendly coworker in Christ that he has been to me. I look forward to get to know Linda better one day when I see her in heaven, but for now, I will say a temporary goodbye to her. Until we see you face to face again in the presence of our Lord Jesus, thank you Linda, for being a blessing to so many, and for being a wonderful witness of Jesus Christ.

Mary Goldwag (Pdf)

Linda was one of the kindest people in the world, and surely one of the most generous. As an extra gift, she was so imaginative in how she could be helpful.

I met Linda through her sister-in-law and my dear friend, Sylvia Jones Turrell. Whenever Sylvia was in town, Linda made a point of inviting my husband, Ed, and me to visit Sylvia in their home. In between times, Linda invited us to her Christmas parties and some of her other parties as well. Linda's Christmas parties were legendary. Only her imaginative planning, careful preparations, and meticulous attention to detail could create such elaborately joyful occasions. No one could have anything other than a great time at Linda's parties, no matter how disparate her guests' interests might be.

Linda's care for people was no once-a-year thing. Throughout the other months, she did more imaginative and generous things, albeit on a (slightly) smaller scale. For example, there was *the sausage episode*, which she dismissed as a minor thing, but which dazzled Ed and me. At one of her summer parties, Ed told Linda that he loved the sausage he was eating. She said she was about to go back to North Carolina to visit friends and family there, which was also where she'd bought the sausage. She'd bring back sausage for Ed, she promised. And she did – quite a lot of it, too. Whenever Ed and I cooked and ate any of it, we lifted our forks in the direction of Linda's and Earle's house (northwest of us by several miles) and thanked Linda for the splendid treat we were enjoying.

Later, when Ed was wrestling with his cancer, Linda arranged for an Edible Arrangement to be delivered to him. Maybe sometime in the vague past, Ed and I had heard of Edible Arrangements, but this was the first (and, so far, only) one either of us had ever seen in real life. That period of Ed's and my life offered many more gray moments than bright ones, but – because Linda arranged it SO — there we were, nibbling on one of the bright moments, disguised though it was as a banana and chocolate-dipped strawberries sprouting from a flowerpot. Again I say, thank you, Linda.

Then, when Ed died, Linda and Earle came to the memorial service. She asked me what she could do to help me. I asked her and Earle to save their newspaper copies of Ed's obituary for me, so I could mail the copies to out-of-town friends and family. Linda and Earle did save them, and I'm still grateful.

It was a joy to know Linda. I'll miss her kindness and generosity, and her open welcome to Ed and me. Most of all, I'll miss her lively, happy spirit. I'm thankful that she and I had the chance to meet and get to know each other somewhat, even though only for a too-short time. She was a blessing in Ed's and my life. And her memory is a blessing in my life now.

With affectionate thoughts of Linda, of both of you, and of the rest of your families,

Mary Goldwag

Liana Leiprichakul

My name is Liana and I have known Linda since 1980. We met at the Pension Benefit Guaranty Corporation as coworkers and became friends. Our friendship began when she encouraged me to take some courses in computer programing. I took her advice and, when the opportunity came, she connected me with the right people who started my career in computer programming. That connection helped my career take off. I am now a retired Federal Insurance Corporation as Computer Database Administrator. I am grateful for what Linda has done for me to start my career.

We were not only coworkers, but we also became friends over the years. Our friendship blossomed after our children were born. Four years after she had Stephen, I had a daughter, Andrea. Linda helped give me advice and guidance on raising a child. I took the classes that she recommended and enrolled Andrea in the same preschool Stephen attended. As our children grew up, we occasionally got together to catch up over dinner and games.

Linda was a wonderful host and loved throwing parties. When Andrea was getting married, Linda help me throw her a wonderful bridal shower. She hosted it at her home and thought up the best activities and games. When I became a grandmother, she gave me the best tips and encouraged me to take a grandparent course to freshen up my child care skills.

We didn't need to talk to each other often or go shopping every weekend to grow our friendship, but we felt comfortable to reach out whenever we needed advice or wanted to share good news. When we did get together, it was special.

I am glad our lives crossed paths and that we became good friends. I will always be grateful for what she has done for me and how we walked life together.

The Nock Family
Robert Nock, Diane Powers-Nock, Cateena and David Powers, Rob Nock, Ani Nock

A Tribute to Linda Eatmon-Jones

By Diane Powers-Nock, Robert Nock, Cateena and David Powers, Rob and Ani Nock

Always present. That is what I love and will always cherish about Linda Eatmon-Jones. No matter whether the occasion was a family gathering, mutual problem solving, or discussing our shared faith, when you were with Linda, you were the only person in the room.

Our bond started the way it does when you are neighbors living on the same street. We shared lots of burgers on the grill, marveled at her landscaping skills, laughed at my lack of a green thumb and shared funny stories about people and places in our lives. Along the way, there were weddings, graduations, and introductions between our two families. It did not take long to realize we shared more than a street address.

Linda was very proud of Steve and Earle. She loved that they loved each other as much as she did. They made a great family.

My husband, Bob Nock and I could not have been happier for them. Earle shared Linda's interest in the next generation. When our teenage son, Rob, almost the same age as Steve, took an early interest in business, Earle mentored him. Linda and I smiled over the dinners they shared and could only imagine what they discussed one-on-one and the wise counsel Earle offered. It must have been pretty good advice, because, like Steve, Rob turned out alright. Later as an adult, Rob took pride in making introductions between Linda, Earle, and Steve to his wife, Ani, and first daughter, Mackenzie. In this way, our bond with Linda was a shared wealth.

In the late 90s, my brother, David Powers (Lt. Col.-USAF), and sister-in-law, Cateena Powers, a businesswoman, then relocated to Northern Virginia from Colorado Springs. It wasn't long before they too fell under Linda, Earle, and Steve's magic touch. Together we attended Antioch and had the pleasure of our two families breaking bread a time or two over brunch after services. Cateena and Linda drew close when she often sat with Linda during chemo when Linda first discovered she had cancer.

Linda, eventually becoming an author, was a great one for putting the right book in your hands when you needed it most. When we lost my father, Winston Powers (Lt. Gen.-USAF), Linda and Earle could not have been kinder. At this time, my now 87-year-old mother too came to know the Eatmon-Jones family too, when he passed. It was a hard loss and I recall reading and re-reading the book Linda brought me, "Chicken Soup for the Soul."

Years later, Bob and I relocated to Glen Allen and were expecting our first granddaughter, Mackenzie. Linda drove from Vienna and presented me with a file folder full of tips and literature on what every new grandmother needed to know.

Often, the big sister that I did not have, Linda's generosity of spirit made it easy to learn from her example. Now, twenty-five years later, I feel my whole family understands the gift that Linda was while here on earth and we will forever hold her memory dear. We plan always to be available to Earle, Steve and their beautiful family.

Carols Palacios
(Translated from Spanish by Carmen Ancieta)

Today, I am going to tell you about a very good and sincere person who was part of my life and who I will always remember for all her advice. I consider her a miracle in my life because she always reminds me that we have a lot to give and learn from others regardless of their economic condition. She taught me to always be a good person with values and good habits that we can acquire in the course of our lives. That is how I met Linda. All my family knew her as a beautiful mom and we remember her with affection and for her generosity with others. That is how I hear today, her advice that guides me on a good path.

One bit of her advice is that we must treat others as we want to be treated, I have known her for ten years and she was always a very charismatic and entrepreneur, mother, wife, writer, friend, and great human being. I always ask her to guide us on the right path. You will live in our hearts as an angel that God sent into our lives to teach us and help us to be better people for others. We always remember you, Linda Eatmon Jones.

Manya Rayner

When I met Linda in the 80s, I was a young professional in the mortgage industry and she held a management position at Fannie Mae (the agency which dictated every move I made concerning mortgages). It was a thrill to meet a Harvard

MBA. I was nervous when I arrived at her office on Wisconsin Avenue in Washington, DC, in my tailored navy blue suit (with shoulder pads, of course). As I waited for our meeting, I wondered what her suit would look like, a high executive at Fannie Mae. I cannot remember at all what she wore because once I saw her face, I saw nothing else. There was a magnetism exuding from Linda's face that would hold me for the next 30+ years. Bright, intelligent, confident, humble–all these things came through her smile. I had never met anyone whose demeanor had such an impression on me. I didn't know then how fortunate I would be to call her a friend for decades to come.

Fast forward through the 90s, the turn of the century, and beyond. Our friendship grew personally and professionally. I remember one particular business transaction. I was having a hard time obtaining something from an agency on Linda's behalf. When I told her, she picked up the phone and called the agency. Without raising her voice or speaking a harsh word, she had the document coming through the fax before she hung up the phone. This was a woman who could always get things done!

When Earle came into her life, I was skeptical, since I really didn't think anyone would be good enough for her. Boy was I wrong – if Linda was the perfect woman Earle was the perfect man. He was the ying to her yang and the most quintessential gentleman I had ever met.

She fell head over heels for Earle and just when I thought no one could love anyone more – his love for her was amazingly beautiful – and well deserved! If anyone loved a woman as much as Earle did, he wouldn't mind putting up 36 Christmas trees for her. Linda and Earle would host the event of the season – an amazing Christmas party. Ray and I had never seen anything like it. Games, food and Christmas cheer galore. Linda and I shared that magical love of Christmas.

Guessing how many Christmas trees were decorated was my favorite game, although I never won. She always had more than my guess.

Through the extravagance of Christmas parties, her formidable business career and in her personal life (good times and rough times), the most impressive thing about Linda was her deep devotion to her faith. That's the one thing that never changed–never wavered, and kept a giant of a woman humble. Earle and Linda shared their great faith and I admired them both for that.

I will always miss Linda. I will never forget her as I feel she influenced me in so many ways. I am sure this happened to many people she knew and, for that reason, her greatness will live on. What a legacy - one not many could claim. That wonderful smile will always live in my mind, making me a little more confident, tolerant, faithful, giving and humble each day. For that, I am so grateful to Linda! May her memory be eternal.

Joshua Rich

I began teaching Linda piano about six or seven years ago. From the minute I first met her, I was struck by her spirit, warmth, humor and graciousness. She was always so attuned to how others were doing, and I was always impressed with her gentle and utterly hospitable manner.

We got to know each other very well, I suppose, as a friendship bloomed out of the piano lessons. She was always frustrated with herself for not progressing faster, not finding time to practice. But she insisted on keeping it in her life since she did derive joy from whatever advances she was able to make at the instrument.

We talked about her family, notably her father, who obviously made a huge impact on her life. We talked about her sisters, her grandchildren, and of course, her son Steve. She was so proud of him and so impressed with the man he became. I know she held such a dear spot in her heart for him. And then, naturally, Earle.

They were such a great couple and I remember always being impressed with their bond and respect and love for one another. I was fortunate enough to be involved in his surprise party that she put together, where I performed the song "Touchstone," that she has commissioned me to compose

for him and for her book. They both were such a force to be reckoned with and together made quite a formidable and loving pair.

Linda was strong, funny, thoughtful, wise, inquisitive, sweet, tough, and possessed a beautiful aura and spirit, which she freely and happily shared with the world, never asking anything in return. In fact, one of the memories I have of her that remains the most vivid is whenever she would do something nice for someone, instead of asking for a thank you, she would insist that we "pay it forward" – that we do something nice for someone else in memory and honor of the kindness she had bestowed upon us.

She was truly one of a kind and will be missed sorely. I am grateful for having had the time I had with her and for the way she touched my life.

Joshua Rich

Cynthia Robbins

It gives me great pleasure to speak on my behalf of an inspiring lady whom I have known for many years.

Linda was a true gift to the people in her life. The way she carried herself was truly admirable. She was so strong. I was so lucky to have known her. She made you see things in an entirely different way. She was a ray of sunshine.

Shiu Family
Leon, Alice, Charlene and Hailey Shiu

Linda Eatmon-Jones was a very special lady. Even though we only met her for few times, our family always remember her as creative, artistic, friendly and energetic. We will never forget her great smile.

- Shiu Family

Charisse Tang

Linda's incredible love for all deeply impacted me. After learning of all her community service, love for others, and powerful example as a wife, mother, grandmother, sister, and friend, Linda is indeed one of my favorite heroes that I aspire to follow.

In particular, from the tributes shared in her beautiful memorial service, I am absolutely amazed by Linda's godly character traits listed below, which serves as an awesome model for all to follow, including myself:

- Accomplished so much for God's glory and still made the time to stop & listen to whoever needed her at that moment.

- -Was a loving mom, sister, friend, and grandmother to so many.

- -Had such a big heart to host gatherings that were filled with so much love, that all wanted to have her coordinate their special events.

- -Had a genuine and deep admiration for her husband, Earle, to write a powerfully moving book about him and his family.

- -Received God's help to work incredibly hard to steer her dear son towards Christ, despite the challenges. Even more so, supporting her son through his faith in Christ, to result in him being a highly impactful pastor.

Linda, THANK YOU for living out such a godly example for us to follow. We see your legacy in Earle, Pastor Steve and his family, and many others whom you've impacted. I have committed to living out your legacy, too.

God bless you, dearest Linda, for being our hero to follow. We deeply love you and have you forever in our hearts!

In Christ's love,
Charisse Tang

Chapter 6

THE NEXT GENERATION

I n His best-selling book *Mentor Leader,* author and Super Bowl-winning coach Tony Dungy outlines the importance of leaders investing in the next generation of leaders and to be willing to lead in such a way that those you influence can eventually replace you. He says that, "The ultimate goal of every mentor leader is to build other leaders."

For many in the corporate world, the goals are as follows: get to the top, step on as many as you can in the process, leave behind those who are weaker and make sure an organization can crumble without you so that they can realize your importance. In the quest to the top of the corporate ladder, investing in the next generation is not prioritized for two reasons: first, the fear that the person will take your job and leave you out in the cold and second, there is no immediate return on investment for the company or the one who is doing the investing. Many of the fruits of the person's labor become evident much later in life or after the person dies.

For my mother, she was constantly interested in investing in the next generation. She learned a lot of lessons in her life, from her stepfather in her childhood, all the way up to her advanced years and she saw it as her own personal mandate to take those lessons learned and "pay it forward" to the next generation. While I was in high school, she volunteered with a program that allowed her to mentor young women in impoverished neighborhoods in downtown DC. These are young teenage women who come from broken homes, many of them racked with drug abuse, absentee parents and fathers who were incarcerated. One such woman she often brought to our house out in a middle class neighborhood where she taught her good virtues and helped set her up for an education and life success. Some may question the decision to introduce people from these situations to your children in your home, but for Linda, she wanted me to see the importance of investing in those who were less fortunate. She became a mother figure to this woman and gave her love and respect and an opportunity at life, something that this woman did not receive during her life.

While I was in college, I remember her meeting with people in our home and elsewhere, counseling them with different problems. One was a young man, not much older than I, who was having problems in his workplace. I do not remember the issue completely, but I do remember her encouraging this young man to be more confident in his workplace and not worry so much about what others would think of him.

Linda would even take in contractors who did work on our home and help them with their business plans. One such contractor was a young man in his late twenties who came and did various jobs around the house, an immigrant from a Central American country who worked hard, but no doubt had an uphill climb in order to achieve financial independence in the northern Virginia-DC area. She took the time to help him develop a business plan, track income and expenses, teach him to work with various technological tools and promote himself in such a way that he can be set apart from other contractors in the region.

The Grandchildren

This book would not be complete without a recollection of how invested Linda was in my children, her grandchildren. To say that Grammy loved and adored her kids is another great understatement, probably more so than any others mentioned in this book. There aren't many words in the English vocabulary that can grasp the lengths to which she would reach nor the sacrifices she would make for her two grandchildren.

First, she would sacrifice her energy. When our oldest was born, Heather, and I were living with her and my stepdad, Earle. She would have no qualms getting up or staying up until the early morning hours to do night feedings and would volunteer that she could do it as many nights as needed. The only reason she didn't do so with our daughter was that she spent much of that time in the hospital and going through chemotherapy treatments. At that age, many grandparents are content to keep their rest and stay in the background, and there's nothing wrong with that, but she loved her grandchildren too much.

Second, she would sacrifice her time. When we moved to Maryland in 2016, which meant that during traffic, our trip could take 90-120 minutes, she still made trips even during high traffic time. She was available for babysitting, not just for a few hours, but overnight and at times multiple nights so that my wife and I could spend time together and help to build our marriage. She constantly made herself available for whatever was needed as it related to the grandkids.

One thing we became used to was "the entourage" at kids sporting events and recitals. Every family at the little league basketball game, or even practice had one maybe two parents, many not involved. Not so with us. A cheering section of two parents, and two grandparents (occasionally four since Heather's parents would sometimes come) were the norm cheering on the kids. The same was true for recitals and even school events. Even with cancer treatments, book signings and other events going on, she made time to be at all of the grandkids important events, even events that most people don't think are that important for kids.

Third, she would sacrifice her resources. Doting grandmother is another statement that undervalues what she spent on the grandkids. There is a room in her house that is informally called "the toy store," because some can mistake it for one, adorned with train tables, art sets, stuffed animals, trucks and airplanes, just to name a few, and every kid who came over to the house could enjoy it. Every time she came to see the grandkids, she came with something they would like, whether a stuffed animal for Rachael, a toy rocket or airplane for Ryan, or anything else their hearts desired. Her material investment went further than just toys, however. She made a decision to dedicate the proceeds from her book royalties to the college fund for her grandchildren, because she believed so much in their development.

Some might mistake this for buying favor, but for her, it was about an investment in the relationship and serving with an others centered mindset. Investing in others was the heart of who Linda was, it was part of her DNA. The older she became, the more time she spent investing in the next generation and there are two essays in this section that will highlight the type of investment she made in others.

Here are the essays from the next generation

Renee McPherson
Dexter Williams

Renee McPherson

I can't believe I am actually sitting here typing about a woman I adore, a woman who taught me so much, a woman that instilled so much within me, inspired me, and motivated me to push and push harder. She taught me to work for what I want. She made sure I was always happy, cozy, and fed. I never left that house empty-handed, down to the day she forced me to take at least one pack of napkins. I am speechless that our beloved mother, sister, friend, mentor, aunty, cousin, and wife has departed from the earth. Surreal, I must say, especially during these uncertain times of COVID-19 2020.

I will never forget how I became a part of the Eatmon and Jones Family. It all goes back to Papa Earle Jones, Mr. Howard University himself, My Alma Mat-a Class of 1995! At the time, I was the Reminisce Coordinator at an assisted living facility and I managed the staff that cared for "Papa Jones." He started off living with the assisted living residents and gave the staff a warm time. Eventually, he moved on upstairs to my floor where he settled in until the end of Life. Being around Papa Jones gave me pleasure. We formed a deep connection some staff would never understand. Here I am, an African American Manager and I finally had an African American resident. Let's just say, he may have gotten quite a bit of special attention from me and a few other Care Managers. Naturally, I formed a bond with his loved ones. It started off with Ms. Linda and Mr. Earle. Once Papa Jones got settled in, I got to meet his beautiful daughter Sylvia and her family as well as Ms. Linda's siblings. Ms. Linda's brother Jeri was my buddy back in the day. Always, we shared laughter, joking, and more laughter. Sylvia and I act like we've known each other forever every time we get together. Her photography skills are amazing.

As for Ms. Linda and Mr. Earle, those two never missed a beat when it came to Papa Jones' care. Frequently visited and were always a phone call away. That can be abnormal when it comes on to the elderly. Fast forward, I reached a road block in my career and was ready to make changes in my life. I wanted to do better...I wanted to be like the "Jones."

This phenomenal woman dressed like no other. Always business casual, never anything less. Clothes finely pressed with perfect creases in her pants (can't forget about her favorite black socks!)

I realized Ms. Linda would be the perfect mentor. One day during one of her visits, I pulled her to the side and asked her for career ladder advice. We decided offsite would be best to discuss my future. Fast forward, I received a warm welcome to come to her home, with my young children to chit-chat. I had two children in elementary school and a baby in diapers.

When I pulled up to the house, I guess I felt like the Fresh Prince of Bel Air. What an amazing feeling at the entrance. The house was beautifully decorated for Christmas and yet she had so many more decorations to be put up. We talked for hours and I poured my heart and soul out to a woman I barely knew. But it felt right. She listened, assessed, and gave her most honest opinion on how I should march forward in life.

The respect level was set. I understood what I needed to do from there. After touring the beautiful home, I expressed my love for the Christmas holiday. I didn't have nearly as many decorations as Ms. Linda. Before leaving, I left with my first set of Christmas decorations that she was ready to "Let Go" of, as she said. Every year moving forward, I always left her house with a trunk full of decorations! Now I need a second house for all these decorations I have collected over the years. Since Christmas decorations meant equally as much to both of us, we formed a special bond. It was an unspoken understanding that we shared decorating together annually.

Starting in early November, Ms. Linda would start her decoration prep. After work and on weekends, I brought my three kids and sometimes my mother would come to decorate. I spent quality time assembling the tiny figurines in Ms. Linda's sacred office every year. Over the years, I watched that space evolve into her Oval Office, where she sat tirelessly writing her best-selling books.

After days and nights of decorating, we knew it was never in vain. This was all a part of the preparation for the Annual Christmas Party. *TALK about FUNNNN!* My kids, family, my friends and I looked forward to this party every year. The house was always well lit up, brightly shining from all the way at the top of the street. As you're pulling up to the lit up driveway you are greeted by valet parking, coat service, greeters, hosts, chefs, and a full staff on deck. After mixing and mingling through the crowded house, you have no choice but to eat and eat and eat some more! Did I forget to mention there was always a bartender available? After happily filling our bellies, we broke out into groups, created and acted out a Christmas-themed skit. During Ms. Linda's administrative preparation of her annual party, she printed out laminated name tags for each guest. Each name tag had a Christmas symbol indicating which team you were assigned to during the party. Best ice breaker ever! Watching the teams prepare a five-minute play in about twenty minutes was hilarious. Designating roles and digging through the prop box was always fun. Judging time: Everyone was a winner no matter if the team came in first, second or third place.

Ms. Linda was not only a role model for me, she also watched my children grow up. Michael, now twenty-five, has so many great memories that he can share. She taught him how to be a man. He never left her house without some type of Life Lesson. Tatiana, now twenty-two, was her *Princess*. She loved her hug up and called her by her own little pet name! Jahziel, now seventeen, was the baby of the bunch when this all started. I will never forget how he would shy away from her in the beginning. She was the first person that told me not to force him to say "Hi" and to give it time so he doesn't hate her later on in life. I

Learned something new because, in my Jamaican household, we are taught to speak to adults, no matter what. She was absolutely correct. The following year, Jahziel gave her a hug on his own! The bond was set from there.

I will miss Ms. Linda and cherish all of the memories she has shared with my family and me.

I will forever be in shock that her presence is no longer here. To Mr. Earle, thank you for sharing your wife with us! To Steve, thank you for sharing your mom with my family and me. She will never ever ever be forgotten. Forever in our hearts.

Love Always,
Reneé M. McPherson

Dexter Williams
Dexter Williams' Statement on Linda

I knew Linda for nearly my entire life, and I am still processing the fact that I will never get to see or speak to her again. She would always call me "Dexter Man," and I am going to miss that. I know that death is a natural part of the life cycle, but it is still painful. I take comfort in knowing that she will no longer experience suffering, and I pray that God continues to heal her family.

Linda had an enormous impact on my life. When I was younger, I would visit my father on the

weekends. Many of those weekends with my dad included spending time at Linda's house. Anyone who knew Linda, knows that she always had a task for everyone, and I was no exception. She typically had me working in the yard, raking leaves or trimming the bushes. It was not too bad, particularly when she paid me a fair wage. I remember not always wanting to do that type of work, but it was hard to say "no" to Linda

(If you knew Linda, then you know exactly what I am talking about). Also, I was a city boy. So, yard work was never on my to-do list. As I became older, I reflected on that experience and realized that she was teaching me about humility and the value of hard work. It is one of the reasons I am so driven and willing to push through obstacles to achieve my goals.

She was one of my biggest supporters throughout my academic career. When I was in elementary school, I played the role of Dr. Martin Luther King, Jr. as part of a skit where I gave his famous "I Have a Dream" speech. Linda was so excited to be there and recorded the entire play. To her, it may have been a simple act, but it meant everything to me. She also came to my high school graduation and cheered me on, and when I graduated from college, she took me out to lunch that summer to celebrate. I remember those small moments because each of them showed me that I was loved.

One of the most important lessons Linda taught me was the value of acquiring knowledge. After

I graduated from high school, Linda treated me to lunch that summer. We talked about our families, summer plans, and the conversation somehow turned to politics. I told her that I did not like Republicans because they were the "bad guys." She asked me what I meant by that and I could not give an adequate or succinct answer. She then asked why I was a Democrat. Again, I could not offer a thoughtful response. Naturally, I was embarrassed, but she used that opportunity to explain why I needed to fully understand what both parties stood for so I can make an informed decision about my political views. At that time, I understood what she was talking about, but I did not fully appreciate it until later in life. I know that it is cliché to say that knowledge is power, but it is one of the most profound and important statements to remember. In many ways, Linda was preparing me for life. Everything that she taught me when

I was younger has helped me navigate the challenges I have experienced. I will always be grateful for her wisdom.

I am at peace with Linda's passing, but I will never forget her. She had an unmatched presence.

I feel blessed to have known her. She will always be in my mind, and, from time to time, I will hear her voice giving me guidance when I need it the most. Thank you, Linda, for everything. I am going to miss you.

Chapter 7
IMPACT ON ME

Throughout this book, you as the reader have seen many different sides of Linda, but you may be wondering, what about me? You might think *you of all people must have something to say, after all, as her only child. You must have a perspective that can match or surpass the depth of any in this book.* The Answer: of course. After all, I am part of the next generation.

Seeing first-hand how Mom lived day in and day out, there are a number of lessons I learned formally and informally, and these are themes that were mentioned throughout the essays. There are five main areas of impact that mom had on me: work-ethic, follow through, approaching difficult situations, becoming an expert and giving and generosity.

WORK-ETHIC

The key to success in anything is work-ethic, and for my mother, it was doubly true. She had many professions throughout her career – computer programmer, people manager, business and finance manager, non-profit director, board member and writer – and in every single one of them she worked as hard as anyone could. Pulling 10-12 hour days were commonplace while I was growing up. There was never a sense of slacking or of doing anything halfway. The one saying I heard often was, "If you are going to do something, do it right," and there is no way one can do it right without working hard and persevering.

If something needed to be done, there was a process, and an expectation that things be done a certain way. Just a few hours before writing this, I finished mowing the lawn. I started to reflect on the manner in which I went about mowing the lawn and the care and precision I took with everything. A job that could have been rushed in less than one hour, I did in two hours. Why? because it's ingrained in my head, "If you are going to do something, do it right." I began to reflect on the thoroughness of raking the excess grass leftover after cutting, making sure every edge is trimmed and weed-whacked to perfection. I make sure every blade I can find and spot on my property has been cut no matter where or how much it grows. I blow away every blade of excess grass left over on a hard, flat surface. I even weed-whack parts of the grass that were unevenly cut or inadvertently overlooked while mowing.

The same is true for cleaning. When I clean the kitchen or vacuum the carpet, there is a way in which it I fell that it has to be done, with precision efficiency and most importantly absolute thoroughness. Clean surfaces that aren't always seen, leave no speck of dust on the counter or the floor. Clean above and beyond even if it is not required at the time. There is an attention to detail that permeates all that I do because it came from my mother, Linda Eatmon-Jones.

In my years growing up, I didn't see my mother in action at work very much, though I could deduce from the number of hours she spent there, she was very hardworking. The yard was where I could see a tangible version of her work ethic

For those of you who knew my mother, you might think decorating and event planning, which is true, but her main passion was gardening. This was her labor of love, and everyone who has seen the yard talks about it, and once about fifteen years ago, this backyard was featured in a very well-known magazine. There were many days spent working alongside her in her passion. While growing up it was a chore, to be honest. I didn't have much interest in work that I felt didn't bring my any fulfillment and didn't help me get good grades or become "cool." But over time, I gained an appreciation for the life skills I learned, such as work-ethic and patience.

Over the years I have watched these plants and flowers grow as if they are my own kids. I remember when we planted the original trees in the backyard, the crepe myrtle and the dogwood right after we moved to our new house while I was high school. I remember painting the stairway down into the wooded retreat area she called the ponderosa and digging the hole for the pond. I also remember her many times coming home with an SUV full of plants and flowers she bought from the nursery and saying, "time to go to work."

I learned a lot of lessons out there. People, would come and enjoy themselves, which is what you want as a host. You want guests to feel at home when they visit. They remark about how much they feel rejuvenated and appreciate the natural feel of the garden and how well organized everything was. But as someone who was able to actively participate in the development of this yard throughout the years, I was able to see a different perspective of what went on behind the scenes, what it took to make all of this happen and keep all of it happening.

Remember, this is someone who would easily work ten to twelve hours per day at your everyday stressful middle-to-upper-level management job, and in the warm months come home to planting bulbs, flowers, plants and trees, and digging holes. In addition to working hard, she worked smart. She would take the time to develop an organizational framework as to how to accomplish everything and find time to teach her offspring how to do the same.

Many of the spring flowers in the garden came from little bulbs that were planted the previous November. When everyone else is wrapping up their season and just going inside to chill for the winter, mom was out here planting spring flower bulbs like Daffodils, and Hyacinths and Tulips. I would always think, "It's November, why plant now?" But come spring, you realize why they had to be planted. I learned a lot of lessons out there about work and preparation and as I put them into practice in my own house, I begin to see with more appreciation the detail and effort she had to put in to the garden to make it look the way that it did.

FOLLOW THROUGH

A close cousin to work ethic is follow-through. When you learn to put in place a disciplined schedule for accomplishing a goal, a natural by-product can be the perseverance to finish that goal. One cold December day in my pre-pubescent years, I was in the front yard stringing lights on shrubs with mom. Every time I think the job was finished, there was another to be done to make sure things were done right. Finally, at the end of the session of putting up Christmas lights, Mom spoke in that usual parental manner of authority, "In life, there is work and there's play, but know that there is more of the former than the latter." That line stuck with me. I didn't know how to interpret it at the time, but over time it has penetrated my approach to everything – in life, if you want to succeed, there is always more work than play.

That attitude helps you get through the tough times in life, to do things when they aren't always appealing. Working in the garden helped me see a glimpse of perseverance and patience. The life of a farmer is not for everybody because it's a life of work. Mom would say, "The ground don't lie. If you do a poor job planting, you will reap a poor harvest, if you do A-level work in planting, you reap an A-level harvest. The ground don't lie."

The beauty of the garden took hard work and patience, no shortcutting.

The key to follow-through is consistency, going every day, whether you want to or not, and whether you feel like it or not. If other things get in the way, you need to push them out of the way to make time for it. Mom would often point out many people who were all talk and no action, and she would say that's because they have no follow through. I would hear them say, "I plan to do this or that," but later find out that the plan never came to fruition. And if mom knew who they are, she would point out that they didn't have the follow through.

That follow-through has helped me to try difficult things and have the perseverance to keep going when times get rough, which I was able to apply while learning a different language. I studied French in high school, but it never really stuck. But in the final years of her life, after I realized that we would be interacting with our French relatives more often, I decided that I would follow through with this no matter how difficult it is. Learning a language that you did not grow up with will test every fiber of perseverance you have, because just when you think you may have turned the corner, you haven't.

I dedicated myself to learning vocabulary, memorizing many words every day, and ordering a French TV station and listening to dialogues in the car on the way to and from work, and while running errands. At the beginning I was lost, but I persevered, truing that the process of perseverance would prove to have results.

Two years into it, the youth group I run at the church took a mission trip to a French-speaking country and I was able to converse with people and occasionally translate things that were said and even held a twenty-minute conversation with one of the residents in French. We also took a trip to see our relatives and my wife and I was able to take an excursion to a place in France where basically no English was spoken and I was able to communicate with locals for whatever was needed. Because I figured that I could do this with French, I decided that since I work in a Chinese church, I should try Mandarin. The curve is a lot steeper than learning French, but the lessons of perseverance live on in me.

I have not always been perfect at this and I still am not, and this lesson, even with such a great role model as my mom, is not easy to learn. There are still unfinished projects at my house, and in life for that matter, that I've wanted to get into, but haven't. However, there are many times where I have applied this lesson and it has worked.

Approaching Difficult Situations

Mom was never afraid of a challenge and she would make that clear to me. She has made two large-scale career changes, to which some might say shows instability, but upon closer observation shows a willingness to take a risk on something you are passionate about and achieve success while doing it. Her first career involved information technology and she progressed into mid to upper-level management. Then she went to Harvard for her master's degree and switched into an almost entirely new field in business strategy and administration. There she achieved success at Fannie Mae where she became division head. In 2002, she sensed another time to change, left her post at Fannie Mae and went back to school at George Mason to obtain her second Master's Degree in Organizational Development. That shift led her into the nonprofit industry where she coordinated six centers giving tax advice for underprivileged families, presided as CEO for three organizations, Fairfax Partnership for Youth, Crisis Link, and the Koinonia Foundation, and served on the board of Child Help.

There was no challenge too difficult for mom. There was always an understanding that you never backed down from a challenge.

That doesn't mean that every single challenge is one that you should take on – one must exercise wisdom in all things that they do, but to take the easy road in all that you do is not part of that wisdom. It is difficult to change a career – let alone twice – and even more difficult to succeed in said career after a change, but for mom, she made the transition appear seamless.

In my own life, I have attempted to apply these principles. During her time running nonprofits she would always have quotes at the end of her emails. One of them was a quote by Ralph Waldo Emerson, "do not go where the path may lead, instead go where there is no path and leave a trail." The goal in life isn't just to be safe, but to take calculated risks. She would tell me to always be trying to improve yourself, and to do so, you always needed to be seeking challenges. Look to do the best thing, not the safe thing. Don't be afraid to learn mistakes but to learn from them.

I went into the ministry out of God's calling, but these words have stuck with me. I chose to pursue a career that none of my parents, grandparents or great-grandparents had any experience with. That's not the safest thing to do. At the point of graduation in college, I had a job offer with my stepdad's company in public relations. I had safety, I knew I had an offer for well-paying job in a highly reputable corporation many months before I graduated. That is not something most college students have an opportunity to possess. I didn't have to search, I didn't have to frantically peruse sites and send in a resume with an application and references to sit in a pile of papers and emails in an HR office and pray that the lottery odds would favor me. But the goal in life isn't to be safe, it's to glorify God. I knew where God had gifted me and where I could have an impact for him and where he wanted me.

Jesus told a story to his disciples, which is found in chapter 25 of the book of Matthew, verses 14-28. He talks about a man going on a journey, who called his servants and entrusted his wealth to them. To one he gave five bags of gold, to another two bags, and to another one bag, each according to his ability. Then he went on his journey. The man who had received five bags of gold went at once and put his money to work and gained five bags more. The one with two bags of gold gained two more. But the man who had received one bag went off, dug a hole in the ground and hid his master's money.

The man who received five bags of gold gained five more. The man with two bags of gold gained two more. In each situation, the master told those two servants, "well done, good and faithful servant." But the man who received one bag and dug it in the ground did not put his master in a good mood. But what does he say? "You should have put my money on deposit with the bankers, so that when I returned I would have received it back with interest."

What's the moral, the main message, of this story? Always be looking for ways to invest in what God has given you, even if it means taking a risk. Anyone who invests money knows that there is always a certain amount of risk involved. You can lose your money, you can make a bad investment or predict success for a fund or business that seems promising only to have it go bankrupt, but that's part of the process. There will always be bumps in the road, challenges in the road of doing what the good Lord has called you to do, but we have to keep moving forward.

There is a difference between being a risk-taker and a gambler and mom was always wise in that manner. There are certain risks one shouldn't take. Before making financial decisions, there was always an analysis of what he had and what we spend before making a large-scale purchase or commitment. Before engaging in any time-consuming activity, there was an examination of the schedule, the reputation of who we were getting involved with, and the likelihood of success in the venture. There was an organized manner in which mom did things, otherwise, she could not have obtained two masters degrees in fields of high difficulty and have risen to the ranks of CEO in so many companies.

Becoming an Expert

All children think that their parents know everything. But for mom, she really did know a lot, because she was a lifelong learner. She was an avid reader and always looked for ways to become an expert on whatever her hands touched. Just three weeks after Rachael's birth I received word that she had to go to the hospital, because she was not feeling well and that her jaw was swollen. She spent a week in the hospital, and during that week as the illness part subsided the doctors said that they were going to conduct a biopsy – where they would take a small piece of your flesh out of you to examine it. There's only one situation where I've ever heard that term used and I thought to myself "I know where this is going, and it's not good."

She ended up being diagnosed with Hodgkin's lymphoma, which is a cancer of the lymphatic system – a network of tissues and organs that help rid the body of toxins, and transport white blood cells that fight infection. *Cancer.* During the course of my lifetime, my mother had never been sick but for the rare, and I mean rare, exception of not feeling well – a typical fever, having a hard time holding down solids, and laying low for the day. It was just that – a day. This, however, was new unchartered territory.

She would need to attend weekly chemotherapy sessions for months and for a while have limited activity. But what does she do? She became an expert on cancer. She made it abundantly clear to me that she was reading books and taking advantage of all of the benefits of the information age. The goal was to be able to dialogue with the doctors and determine for herself, the best possible treatment options. Was she going to become smarter than the doctors? Of course not, there is no way one can match eight years of formal medical education, two to three years of residency and decades of real-time on-the-job experience by reading books, pamphlets and searching the web in your spare time. But she knew that at the end of the day, it's her body and she needed to discern if it was being treated the right way. Someone from the field of business and computer science learned principles of medicine in order to better understand her condition.

Right before our oldest was born, Heather, my wife and I, moved back into her house and embarked on a project of renovating an unfinished section of the basement, since it had only one bedroom at the time. The goal was to create a bedroom with a closet and bathroom access. The day before the contractor was set to arrive, mom took me aside and schooled me on which drills and saws, and other tools were needed, and said "You want to know what you are talking about when you interact with these individuals so that they don't take advantage of you. If you don't know what tools they are using and the exact tools needed for each job, you can't tell if they are going to ruin your living space." Even though I wasn't doing the job, contractors were, it was still important to become an expert on what they were doing, because she was a lifelong learner and always sought to become an expert.

Mom always spoke of having a knowledge base that is well-rounded. I have sought to apply these principles in my own life. A few years ago I started exploring how to make videos. Way back at the end of high school, in the summer between senior year and freshman year, I had a mini-internship at my step-dad's company where he worked as general manger. I saw a glimpse of video-editing as I helped the promotions team film commercials and figured that this wasn't as difficult as I thought, so I downloaded another more complex software program that can allow you to do more. I started making some mock videos to test my capabilities.

My boss wanted to find creative ways to advertise the church prayer meeting to a younger audience since they were not attending in large numbers. I knew from the visual nature of many teens and 20 somethings that videos could capture their attention and because I had software I could make a video, so I volunteered to do the project. I still had a lot to learn but I put my skills to work, looked up other tutorials, even took a mini-class, and was able to make a 3-minute video that caught the eye of the younger generation and got some of them to come out to the meeting.

I continued working with the software and was able to make a promo for a youth event that exhibited more complex func-tions, and another one that was shown as a promo video for a retreat. I am not a video editor by nature, but I took the time to develop expertise because I believed that it could come in handy. When the coronavirus hit and the church quarantine started, I was able to use the skills developed from using the video editing software to record sermons, and imbed object illustrations and graphics. I could still hear the resounding echo from mom during my adolescence, "Don't pass it off, become an expert of as much as you can, versatility is one of the greatest assets."

I applied the same concept to music. I learned how to play piano at a young age. I was not that interested in the lessons and didn't practice very rigorously, so I decided to play the drums when the opportunity to participate in the band came in the fifth grade. I worked harder at that mainly because of the com-petition at school, which provided a built-in desire to be the best. I went back to piano in two separate spurts only to later quit for lack of desire.

In high school, I started playing drums and percussion even more, playing in the symphonic concert band, the marching band my first two years of high school and playing for the gospel choir at church. My junior year, a friend and I started learning guitar just fooling around while learning Green Day songs. I took to learning chords and progressions and while listening to Christian Contemporary music, I discovered that it's possible for me to learn how to play the guitar to these songs. From the guitar I learned that I could play bass since a lot of it is just learning the low note on the guitar. By the time I got to college and chose to major in music my first two years before switching, I had enough theory classes to have a more intricate understanding chords, their structures and how to create and feel not just the rhythm but the mood and atmosphere of songs and improvise.

To bring everything full circle, the Baptist collegiate ministry, an organization I was heavily involved with in college, took a missions trip to Alabama, where they would conduct revival services at a church for a week. The group of nine who went were in need of musicians to play during the praise and worship time and in particular needed a piano player. Because of what I learned in music theory classes and my experience from childhood, I volunteered to be the piano player. I don't know if it was the ease of playing what seemed to be easier songs than Tchaikovsky or Beethoven, or the fact that the songs meant more to me because of their messages, probably a mixture of both, I started playing piano in a much greater capacity, hence developing more proficiency.

Mom would always tell me when I would go on a hiatus from playing an instrument to keep playing, or find some way to keep that skill honed. The versatility I developed from these four instruments allowed me to always have a role in a praise band at church for decades. I have played all of the four (bass, guitar, percussion, piano) in various forms throughout the years in church settings, and even a few times outside of it. I keep remembering the example to not back down from a challenge and to become an expert as much as you can.

Giving and Generosity

If there was any trait that could define Linda Eatmon-Jones in one word, it would be generosity. Mom was always a very generous person who would give anything to make sure that everyone around her was cared for. Hosting Events, Mentoring, giving to the homeless shelter, giving free things to everyone who comes to the house, taking in people who were in difficult situations were just a few things that characterized her attitude toward others.

While I was in the seventh grade, mom decided to gather the family together around the Christmas holiday. It wasn't on the actual day itself, but it was an occasion to get all of the close relatives together. Knowing my mother, this couldn't stay as a simple gathering.

As we moved to a new house, the gathering began to grow. Gradually more and more friends started coming as the social circle began to expand and by the time I got to college, it started to resemble a major event with ornate decorations at every turn, a caricature artist, catered food and games. For the games, she decided to give prizes and gifts for everyone who attended, which at times exceeded 100 people. Everyone who attended became aware of the famous holiday games, whether they be Christmas carols, skits or other holiday-themed fun. Three judges were appointed to judge the winning team and everyone who attended received a prize, whatever their finish. And these gifts were not merely party favors – board games, wine, meat and cheese packages, movie gift cards. With Mom, you always go all out for others.

One could argue that with sufficient income, gestures like the one in the previous paragraph are relatively easy. Many people give out of their wealth, but few are willing to make uncomfortable sacrifices to help those in need.

While I was in college, I would always come back home during breaks and attend the college service at church. This particular summer I was able to be placed in a small group Bible study that met for a few weeks while I was in town, along with some other college students in the same situation. During the time where we normally share prayer requests, one of them mentioned having a difficult living situation, and continued to elaborate on the extremely controlling and manipulative nature of the individual with which this student resides. I could see the trepidation in this student's voice grow as he continued to pontificate on the situation, and the atmosphere in the room began to collect more and more anxiety. The night the meeting was over, I went to mom and Earle and asked if a man I had only known for a couple of weeks, whom I had barely met and they have never seen, could live with us for a few months. They gave their blessing and I relayed it to the student who was beyond relieved to know that he could make an exit from his tenuous situation. The risk paid off, the experience worked out wonderfully, I made a lifelong friend and we were groomsmen at each other's weddings.

OVERALL IMPACT

I have only given a sliver of the impact that Linda made on me. There is an array of life lessons that take place in any mother-child relationship and I do not have the time to delve into every single situation that reflects the full nature of the impact she made on my life. Mom lived a full life and it was her priority that people be well-rounded and excel in all facets of life: spiritual, emotional, career and family, to name a few.

EPILOGUE

"Success is not measured in the amount of dollars you make, but the amount of lives you impact." (Anonymous)

This quote has defined the way Linda Eatmon-Jones has lived her life and it has been evident through the essays you have just read. In the Bible, in the book of 2 Timothy, a book that the great apostle Paul penned to his protégé Timothy from an Ephesian prison awaiting death, he gave some very pertinent life lessons since he knew he was passing the torch. In the final chapter of the book, chapter four, he gives instructions on preaching the gospel and not turning aside to those who selectively choose preachers who "say what their itching ears want to hear." But then he turns the attention to himself in verse 6.

> *For I am already being poured out like a drink offering, and the time has come for my departure. I have fought the good fight, I have finished the race, I have kept the faith. Now there is in store for me the crown of righteousness, which the Lord, the righteous Judge, will award to me on that day—and not only to me, but also to all who have longed for his appearing.*

For almost every application for jobs, for ministries and including seminary, a question is asked "what is a verse that defines your life – a life verse?" And to almost every time this question has been asked on an application, my response has been these three verses – 2 Timothy, Chapter 4, verses 6-8. It is an inspiration in part because I have seen my mother live this way and this was her legacy to me and many others – one of Christian example.

Paul states his legacy in these verses and to say that his legacy was one of impact on others is the understatement of the year. Formerly a man who persecuted Christians and celebrated their gruesome deaths, he met Jesus on the road to Damascus in a vision and from that point on became Christianity's greatest defender. He authored almost half of the books of the New Testament, led countless people across the Roman Empire to faith in Jesus Christ and helped to start churches in well-known cities of the time such as Corinth and Ephesus. His story and works are read from church pulpits on every continent most every Sunday, despite the fact that his life was one that we in the current day would call one of great suffering. When I look at my mother's life and consider how she ran the race and fought the good fight, I think about two things, energy and endurance.

ENERGY

Paul says in verse 7 of the same chapter, "I have fought the good fight." In this life, there are plenty of fights to fight. From time to time, I speak and lead Bible studies at Fellowship of Christian Athletes meetings at local high schools. When I walked through the halls of one particular school, I noticed that there are all kinds of causes to support. Give blood, stand up for this political cause or that political cause, help disadvantaged people. There are so many causes to support. Social justice is a big deal in our society, that's why the term SJW (social justice warrior) was invented recently to describe people who have a particular passion for these kind of social justice causes.

These things are good, I'm not saying in any way that we shouldn't help our brother or our sister or our neighbor who is in a situation of physical or emotional need – we should. But we have to be focused in what we do, something has to take precedence. For Paul, that something was the gospel – the good news that Jesus Christ is the Savior of the world, that though we are sinners, we are not perfect. We are separated from a holy powerful and loving God because of our sin, Jesus, who is fully God and fully human, came to the earth and lived a perfect life. And because he is fully God and fully man, his death is suffi-cient to satisfy the penalty and pervasiveness of sin in our lives if we trust him, confess our sins to him and make Him our Lord. That is the fight that for Paul took precedence over every fight.

You may not be a Christian if you are reading this, so the gospel message may not be something to which you feel you should devote your energy and that's okay. But I believe that to have a life of impact you must focus your energy. When everything is of utmost importance, nothing is. When you dilute your energy to too many things, you will lose the ability to make the biggest impact you can, to leave the best legacy you can, the impact of the power of the gospel in the lives of people.

For Linda, her energy was focused. She did a lot and accom-plished a lot in life, but it was based in the values of investing in family and relationships. Many people have goals to become rich, to have the best house in the nicest neighborhood, to have the most decorated linked-in profile, develop exotic hobbies, or to travel the world. But none of those goals will create long lasting impact. After you die, someone else will inherit your house and your money, and accomplishments, unless they are built on investing in the lives of others, will be forgotten. As I read through these essays, I noticed how little attention was paid to my mother's Harvard degree, the size of the house or the titles she held in the workplace, even for those who worked for her. What stood out is the relationships she created and those in whom she invested.

Our energy is a limited resource – use it wisely. When everything is of utmost importance, nothing is. Make sure you know which fight you are fighting and in whom you are investing.

ENDURANCE

Paul says, still in verse 7, "I have finished the race, I have kept the faith." For Paul, he didn't just fight the good fight, he fought it all the way through to the end. He finished. He didn't just do it sometimes, or when it was convenient. He didn't quit, he went all the way to the end.

And it's not like his race of keeping the faith was an easy one. Most people think of Paul as a hero of the faith who preached and healed everyone he came in contact with and got the honor of writing half of the New Testament, a celebrity of sorts. Those things are true, but the bible records many examples of suffering that Paul went through. Here are some, just to name a few:

- In Antioch, there was a severe famine.

- In Iconium, they plotted to stone Paul and Barnabas after they preach and though many got saved, they were run out of the city.

- In Lystra, he actually does get stoned and left for dead after doing the exact same thing.

- In Philippi, he and Barnabas cast a demon out of a woman and they get stripped down, flogged and thrown into prison.

- When he came to Jerusalem, the beating he took from the initial arrest was so severe that soldiers had to carry him and even while being questioned, there was an underground plot on his life that forced him to be shipped to Caesarea.

- When he was sent to Rome to appeal to Caesar, he became shipwrecked in a violent storm. When they came ashore to an island called Malta, he was bitten on the hand by a viper in what normally is a fatal snakebite, but God spared him.

- And of course, not to forget the fact that he was in prison as of the writing of this letter and eventually got beheaded.

Look at all that this man went through and yet still finished the race, still kept the faith. So many times he was knocked down, so many times he was treated unfairly, so many times he endured suffering and persecution for a message he believed in, and yet he still persisted in making sure everyone he came in contact with received this message.

My mother went through some rough patches in her life. Her own birth and upbringing as an illegitimate child in a small town was one, her divorce was another, and from accounts from those close to me, the death of her stepfather when she was just twenty-nine years old was another. There were probably countless others I was just not made aware of in order to protect me. These are situations that can break many people for my mother she endured.

If you want to have impact, you must be willing to endure and finish well. This is an example I strive for in my own life, to not be kept down by difficult situations, but always look for the silver lining and message God is trying to send to me and to move forward. There will always be tough situations throughout life, and that is the case whatever your race, socio-economic status, hometown, job title or how much cash you have in your retirement account. They key is how do you endure through these trials. Are you able to stay focused on your mission despite the difficult situations you face?

Forbes magazine put out an article a few years ago titled *The 25 Biggest Regrets In Life. What Are Yours?* At the top of the list? Working so much at the expense of family and friendships.

Lives of impact are based in investment of others and living out an example of virtues like love, peace, joy, patience and kindness, especially among those close to you. You can build bridges that last hundreds of years, you can build businesses that last generations, you can start movements that outlast your tenure. But no legacy will carry like a life of investing in others.

EARLY LIFE

FAMILY PICTURES

At her famous Christmas party with her granddaughter

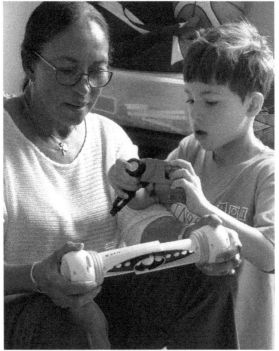

Linda with her grandson

Linda with her granddaughter

Linda with her mother, husband Earle and father-in-law

At the birth of her first grandchild with Earle, myself and my wife Heather

ACKNOWLEDGEMENTS

- I would first like to thank my Lord and Savior, Jesus Christ.

- I would like to thank my beautiful wife for having patience with me while I composed this work, believing in me, trusting in me and being my proofreader and giving the advice needed to help this work from a good literary work to a great literary work. You challenged me to go beyond what I knew was possible and saw what I could not see.

- I would like to thank my stepfather Earle and my father, James Eatmon, for having faith in me and believing in me when it was difficult to believe in myself. You two are truly a blessing to me and your investment in me cannot be quantified. That same is true for your grandchildren.

- I would like to extend an extremely deep heartfelt thanks to all those who have submitted an essay. It was extremely touching and moving to read your heartfelt sentiments and learn about the way which she impacted your life. This was a much a learning experience for me as it was an emotional experience for me, especially those who knew her while I was little. My hope is that this experience has given you an opportunity to find some kind of closure and express your thoughts and feelings. The pandemic has made grieving a difficult experience for all of us but my prayer is that this opportunity can help.

- I would like to thank the team at Xulon press for the opportunity to publish this book and take a chance on me as a first-time writer. You all have so wonderfully guided me through this process and turned this project into a work of art.

References

1. Linda Eatmon-Jones, *Thank You Daddy,* Maitland, FL: Xulon Press 2018) xx.

2. "Forty facts about two parent families," Gillespie Shields, 2019, accessed December 29, 2020, https://gillespieshields.com/40-facts-two-parent-families/.

3. "10 key findings about the religious lives of U.S. teens and their parents," Pew Research Center, September 10, 2020, accessed December 29, 2020, https://www.pewresearch.org/fact-tank/2020/09/10/10-key-findings-about-the-religious-lives-of-u-s-teens-and-their-parents/.

4. Linda Eatmon-Jones, *Touchstone,* (Denver: Outskirts 2016), 3.

5. "The Black Family Is Struggling, and It's Not Because of Slavery," The Daily Signal, September 20, 2017, accessed December 20, 2020, https://www.dailysignal.com/2017/09/20/black-family-struggling-not-slavery/.

6. "Census Bureau: Higher Percentage of Black Children Live with Single Mothers," The Black Media Authority, December 31, 2016, accessed December 30, 2020, https://afro.com/census-bureau-higher-percentage-black-children-live-single-mothers/.

7. Tony Dungy with Nathan Whitaker, *Mentor Leader,* (Chicago: Tyndale House 2010), 188.

CPSIA information can be obtained
at www.ICGtesting.com
Printed in the USA
LVHW071959270621
691281LV00020B/2971